ROLLING STOCKS
and
COVERED CALLS

Two Powerful and Profitable Investing Methods for
Riding the Stock Market's Waves

GLAISTER WELSH

ISBN: 978-0-99876-216-6

To: My loving wife Crystal and our four children
Jabari, Jared, Jace and Jadyn

CONTENTS

ACKNOWLEDGMENTS

I have always admired anyone who could focus long enough to write a book. Each time I walk into a bookstore or library, I am always in awe at the volume of work at our disposal. At first, writing a book seemed both daunting and overwhelming, but as I got into the project, it became more interesting as a snowball effect of ideas took hold. I want to thank those who mentored and encouraged me to take it one step at a time. I want to thank my family for their support, patience and understanding, especially my wife who kept showing me the quote by *Goethe* "What you can do, or dream you can, begin it. Boldness has genius, power and magic in it".

Regarding inspiration for this book – I want to give a big shout-out to the following people who, in their own strange way, have inspired me through the years:

My mom, my dad, my sister Petra, my brothers Ken and Dean and to all those foundation people who gave me courage to step up my game; Jafa, Bruce Lee, Whimpy Brown, BG, Foggy, Putty Locks, Marcus Aurelius (Brutus), Markus Kameka, Woody, Briggs, Massive, Raspa, Ginga and Bigga Brad who once told me "Sitdown naw say gittup".

If you are a part of the fraternity that understands the cheer "Bo Bo Ski Watten Tala Ala Ski Wa" then, in your own way, you have inspired me by your brotherly love and your "can-do" attitude.

And lastly, much love to my HU and DMV family well, "you know" of course that I could never leave you out.

INTRODUCTION

2016 will probably be remembered as a year that produced some of the most remarkable surprises in our recent history. Many of our friends are still shocked by the incredulity of it all. They are still recovering from the Brexit vote, Donald Trump's election, the English Premier League's Leicester City remarkable win and lastly Bob Dylan's Nobel prize in literature. It is difficult to find people who were not overwhelmed by the frequency and magnitude of these events. In the cases of the Brexit vote and the US elections, there is no shortage of analyses and Monday morning quarterbacking. Maybe Thomas Piketty was onto something in his prescient and voluminous treatise on the unequal distribution of wealth and its effect on social and economic stability. In short, it appears people are dissatisfied with the economic and political elites and are finally rising up to stake their claim of the widely touted yet elusive America dream.

Presidential elections will come and go, markets will rise and fall and even soccer teams will win and lose some championships (Go Chelsea). How then will you navigate these cycles, the unpredictable turns and the events due to the vagaries of life? Do you have a road map to understand what it all means? Do you have the tools at your disposal to ensure that you successfully navigate and decipher these ups and downs? How will you position your time and your resources to maximize the returns for your family and for future generations? We do not profess to have all the answers; however, this book provides some insightful tips and useful strategies to navigate the ups and downs of the financial markets.

There are those among us who subscribe to the idea that financial markets know best. Economists call these people rational market adherents because they believe that financial markets possess a certain wisdom that mere mortals do not. On the other hand, there are those people, like Warren Buffett, who believe that the markets are not always efficient and that price inefficiencies exist in the market. In fact, Buffett once proclaimed, "I'd be a bum on the street with a tin cup if the markets were always efficient." These two conflicting schools of thought are each brimming with brilliant scholars and with an abundance of intellectual firepower. Strangely enough, they both have mountains of data to support and rationalize their hypotheses. The most prominent among them, and probably the leading voices for each camp, are Nobel Laureates Eugene Fama and Robert Shiller. Economists - such as the late Irving Fisher, Paul Samuelson and Milton Friedman - have long argued the merits of the rational market. On the other hand, Lawrence Summers, Robert Shiller and, a much later convert, Fisher Black have long critiqued the efficient market hypothesis.

As an individual investor, should you care that these intellectual powerhouses and Ivy League university educated PhDs' are constantly talking from both sides of their mouths? The mere fact that these erudite finance and economics professors cannot come to a conclusion after examining mountains of available evidence should be proof enough that there is room for some alternate hypotheses. If they had all the answers, one would think that they would apply their theories to the market and make some real money. I believe it was Lawrence Summers, the former Treasury Secretary, brilliant economist, failed university administrator and top economic adviser to President Barack Obama, who once asked, "How many finance professors are included in the Forbes 400?"

Do we give these financial engineers and economists more credit than they actually deserve? Long before the market crashes of 1987 and 2007, the idea of the "smart money", referring to the Wall Street elites, was a prominent term in our lexicon. In fact, it was the term du jour for the talking pundits, and financial journalists. Today, that term has slowly disappeared from our verbal discourse. Many people, including the former Chairman of The Federal Reserve Allan Greenspan, were humbled by the financial turmoil in 2007. In the aftermath of the 2007 financial debacle, Greenspan struggled to explain what had gone wrong. Ayn Rand has been long gone and, moreover, the intellectual edifice and assumptions that shaped his thinking could not explain the markets' actions.

In Justin Fox's book *The Myth of the Rational Market*, he mentions that when Bill Sharpe (those people in the finance world will recognize this name due to the Sharpe ratio named after him) was asked about the cause of the October 1987 market crash, his retort was, "It's conceivable that a change in the well-informed forecast of future economic events moved the market as it did, on the other hand, it's pretty weird."[1] Yes, that's exactly what he said. You may also recall that in 1993, Meriwether and Rosenfeld formed Long Term Capital while Merton Miller and Nobel Laureate Myron Scholes signed on as partners. These men were the original quants and the crème de la crème of financial engineering. Long Term Capital is the source of Roger Lowenstein's book *When Genius Failed* due to their epic failure. In his book, Lowenstein dryly noted, "If Wall Street is to learn just one lesson from the Long-Term debacle, it should be that the next time a Merton proposes an elegant model to manage risks and foretell odds, the next time a computer with a perfect memory of the past is said to quantify risks in the future, investors should run—and quickly—the other way".[2]

According to these professors, there are two groups of people who trade or invest in the markets; on one hand you have the smart money and on the other; the idiots or noise traders. The smart money trades use all pertinent available information while the idiots trade on noise as if it were information. Which camp are you in? Do you believe in this market dichotomy? If you believe the professors, none of us regular main street individual investors would ever consistently make money in the market. However, I can assure you that there is a guy somewhere in Wichita, KS or Omaha, NB who gets up every day and is trading in his living room and in his underwear and is consistently making money.

This book is about finding your own path to successful trading (it is a self-help book). In this short paragraph, you will understand the essence of this book. After twelve years of researching and reviewing thousands of rolling stocks, I have selected the top 23 rolling stocks to put in this book (see Case Studies). I have decided to share my methods. First, simply find a reliable list of rolling stocks. Secondly, filter your list (this is where you need to do some homework). I will quote Warren Buffett "Only buy something that you'd be perfectly happy to hold if the market shut down for 10 years" (that says it all). Exercise patience and persistence until you find the right price. I suggest setting price alerts so that when your stocks breach your price points, you will be ready to buy. Before you execute your trades, determine your exit strategy and profit targets. Lastly, sell when you have achieved your profit targets and repeat the process, either on the same stock or on your next favorite stock. That's it. Yes, it's that simple. You do not need to be well-heeled, blue-blooded, pedigreed and the beneficiary of a trust fund to make money in the market - all you need is a solid strategy, confidence and patience.

One very last word (and this is advice I also share with my kids). Since most of us do not save enough, I cannot resist the urge to encourage you to save at least 10% of your income in an IRA, 401K, 403B or any other type of retirement plan. You should start on the very first day you start your new job. If you are working and have not started saving, please start today – it is the gift that keeps on giving. By buying this book you are taking the pledge to start investing in your future today.

CHAPTER 1

Rolling Stocks - A Brief Overview

What are rolling stocks? By definition, a rolling stock offers at least three buying opportunities in a 12-month period which will each yield as least a 10% return. Rolling stocks move between a support price point (sometimes referred to as the floor) and a resistance price point (referred to as the ceiling). When these stocks visit the price point at the floor level – it is time to pick them up (buying opportunity). When they rise to the ceiling, it is typically the time to sell. Do they always strictly roll for 12 months? Sometimes they roll for much longer and some rolling stocks may roll for shorter than 12 months. However, our criteria dictate that a stock that rolls for 12 months should be considered a rolling stock. Will you always generate a 10% gain with each trade? It is highly unlikely. In most cases, you will not get to buy at the absolute bottom of the roll (floor) and similarly, you may not get to sell at the absolute top of the roll; however most people would not complain if they got a positive gain on each trade – whether that is 2% or 8%.

Let's do some quick back of the napkin math to see what this could mean to you. I will use some real numbers in an example below to illustrate how a rolling stock can have a positive impact on your portfolio.

- Stock Support Price................$28.00
- Stock Resistance Price..............$34.00
- Difference $6.00
- Annual Gain........................64% (this return calculation assumes 3 round trip trades per year and does not take transaction costs into account)

A brief example of an actual trade will drive home this point. We identified Whole Foods Market (WFM) as a rolling stock early in its life cycle and started trading the stock. The table below demonstrates the trades made over a period of several months. Not accounting for the trading transaction costs, these three trades resulted in a 62% net gain.

Rolling Stock Trades – Whole Foods Market (WFM)

	Roll 1	Roll 2	Roll 3
Month	Jan 2016	May 2016	Sept 2016
Entry Price	$28.10	$28.20	$27.80
Exit Price	$34	$35.00	$32.50
Gain	$5.90	$6.80	$4.70
% Gain	**21%**	**23.9%**	**16.90%**

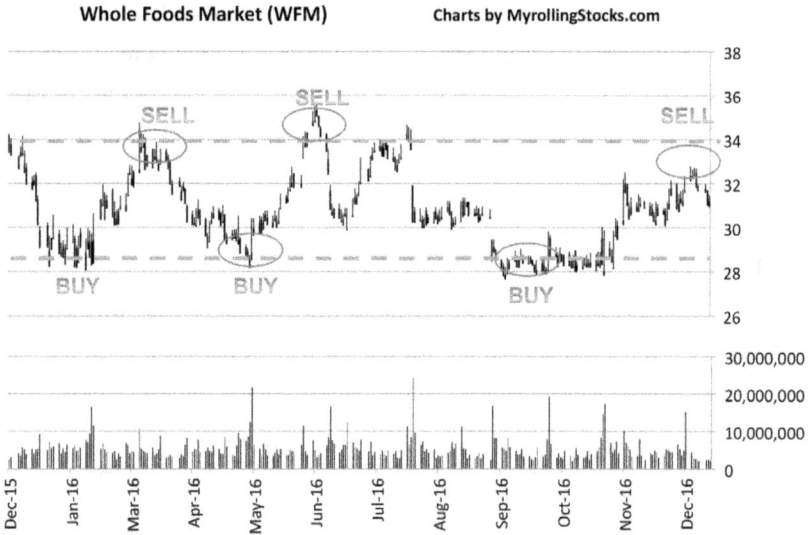

Whole Foods Market (WFM) — Charts by MyrollingStocks.com

As you may have realized from the example, we are not overly concerned with buying at the absolute bottom and selling at the top. Quite frankly, we do not know where the top and/or the bottom will be. We are using our best judgment and the past performance of the stock to predict its future movement. The illustration shows that if you had bought at the support and sold later at the resistance your annual gain would have been 62%. That gain in anyone's portfolio is not too shabby.

After reading this book, you will know where to find rolling stocks and you will be able to identify scenarios where budding rolling stocks exist. You will then use the skills and technique you will learn from this book to be able to get into the stock at the right price level. Just like a surfer who has to catch a wave at the right speed before jumping onto a wave, you will also need judgment and skill to determine the right price levels to jump into a rolling stock. The parallels to wave surfing can be extended even further. There are many input variables necessary for the successful execution of a surfing routine. Similarly, there are multiple variables that are required for trading rolling stocks (some people actually call them wave stocks). With surfing, the surfer has to use judgment and intuition to match the speed of the wave. She then has to balance the forces of gravity, buoyancy, the hydrodynamic forces exerted on the surf board by the water and the kinetic energy. If the surfer gets all these variables correct, she can smoothly navigate and ride the waves all the way to the shore.

Just as the surfer is negotiating with hydrodynamic and buoyancy forces, the rolling stock trader is attempting to navigate market forces. In so doing, she is trying to determine the timing of the trade and the optimal price levels. In some cases, if a rolling stock is not worth a trade, she will wait for the right stock at the right price. Market forces are driven by variables which include the intrinsic value of the stock, that is, the capital equipment, cost of goods sold, inventories, profits, and the actual stock market data, including the mean prices over time and variances to the mean stock price. One of the most important variables driving these market forces is the psychology of the market (the actions of the crowd). The trader must use skill, experience and intuition to successfully navigate the entry point into a stock and to successfully identify the best entry point.

"If principles can become dated, they are not principles." - *Warren Buffett*

Once you have mastered the techniques of trading rolling stocks and you become proficient at making money, then you can move on to other strategies. In later chapters, we cover options and covered calls. The transition from rolling stocks to options and covered calls will become easier once we understand the basics of trading rolling stocks.

"If I had known then what I know now – I would have made the same mistakes sooner." – *Robert Half*

CHAPTER 2

What I Learned About Rolling Stocks

Rolling Stocks are More Commonly Found in Lower Price Ranges

Rolling stocks occur when a stock is trading in a sideways channel for at least 12 months. Do they occur more frequently at lower price points? The data below represents more than 3800 rolling stocks collected over an 8-year period. The data is not normally distributed and is skewed to the left of the graph. This data supports the hypothesis that most rolling stocks occur in lower price ranges. This data shows that 47% of rolling stocks occur under the $10 price range. In the data population of over 3800 stocks, there were 11 stocks that were above the $70 price level. In his 1998 book *Rolling Stocks – Making Money On the Ups And Downs*, Gregory Witt made the claim that rolling stocks are more commonly found in the lower price ranges.[3] The data presented in the chart below supports that argument.

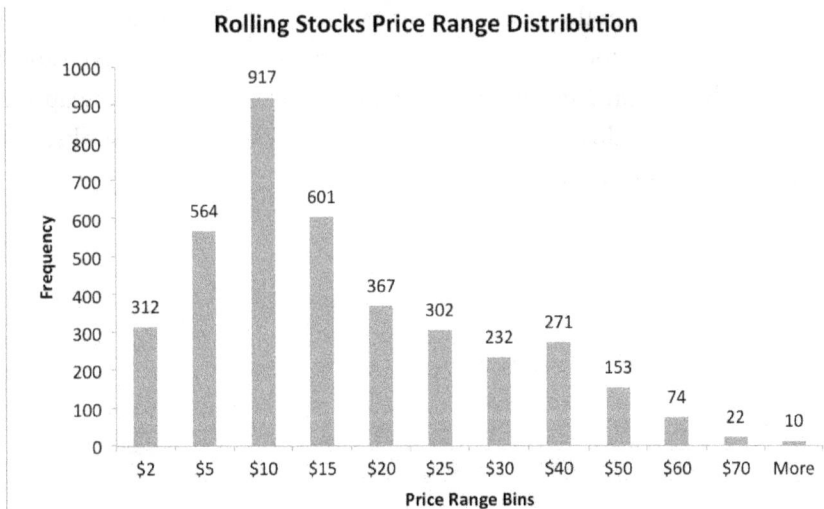

Rolling Stocks Price Range Distribution

Price Range Bins	Frequency
$2	312
$5	564
$10	917
$15	601
$20	367
$25	302
$30	232
$40	271
$50	153
$60	74
$70	22
More	10

"If you think you can, you can. If you think you can't, you are right." – *Mary Kay Ash*

Lower Price Stocks Roll Faster

Do lower price stocks roll faster? It would be fantastic if we could get in and out of a stock in a week or even a month and generate the same 10 to 15% that we targeted. After reviewing all the data on rolling stocks and comparing stocks in the $1.00 to $10.00 range to stocks in the $15.01 to $25 range, we found that the lower priced stocks do tend to roll faster. What does this mean for you? If you found a stock that was priced lower and rolling faster, should you buy the stock? There are many opportunities where the duration of the roll from support to resistance is days instead of weeks. We tend to find more of those opportunities in the lower priced stocks.

Rolling Stocks Tend to Break-out After They Finish Rolling

Rolling stocks can remain in a sideways rolling pattern for months or even years. What typically happens when they break-out of that sideways pattern? Do they go up in price or do they fall in price? As we noted previously, very few people have been successful at predicting the direction of stocks. We can simply talk about the probability of an event happening. In the case of rolling stocks, our data suggest that these stocks tend to break-out to the upside. When rolling stocks breakout, there is a statistically significant difference in the proportion of rolling stocks that break out to the upside than those stocks that do not. We examined over 412 rolling stocks that had a break out. The majority (79.5%) of them broke out to the upside. The graphs below illustrate a few examples of stocks that have broken out of their rolling pattern to the upside.

GBLI - Global Indemnity Ltd Charts by MyRollingStocks.com

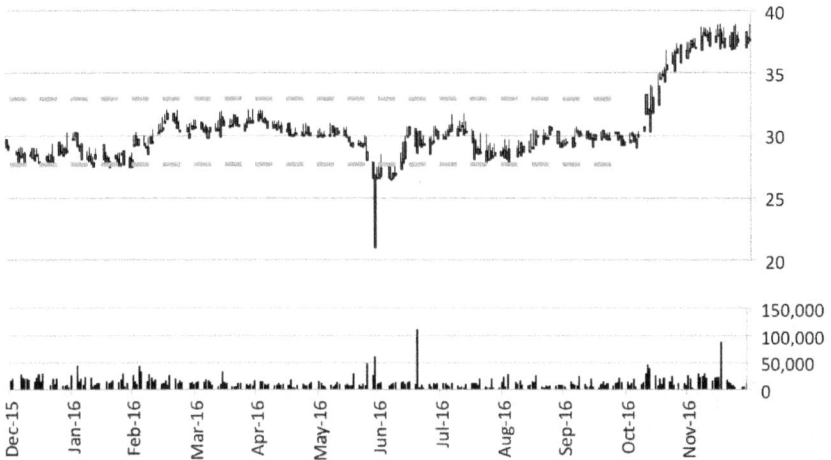

Global Indemnity Plc., (GBLI) is a holding company. The company offers an array of insurance and reinsurance products and services to a range customer base. For the greater part of one year, the stock was rolling between a support of $27.50 and a resistance of $32.00. In mid-November 2016, the stock broke out of this rolling pattern and most recently has been trading in the mid-$37 price range. This is an example of a stock that has successfully broken out of a narrow trading range.

Westamerica Bancorporation (WABC) - Charts by MyRollingStocks.com

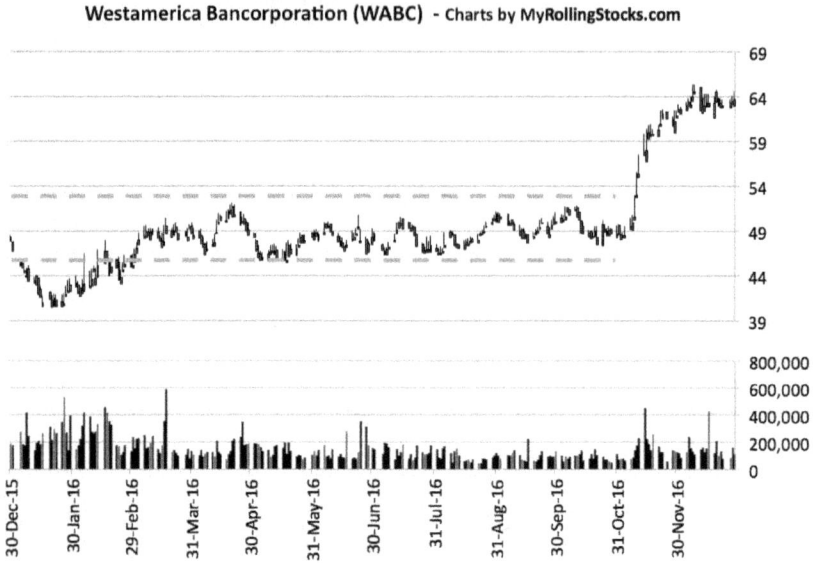

Westamerica Bancorporation (WABC) is a bank holding company. The company provides a range of banking services to individual and corporate customers in Northern and Central California through its subsidiary bank, Westamerica Bank. This is another example of a stock that traded between a support of $45 and $51 for most of the year. In a similar fashion to the previous example, this stock broke out to the upside and recently traded in the $62 price range.

First Financial Northwest Inc (FFNW)   Charts by MyRollingStocks.com

First Financial Northwest, Inc. (FFNW) is a holding company for First Financial Northwest Bank (the Bank). The Bank's business consists of attracting deposits from the public and utilizing these funds to originate one- to four-family residential, multifamily, commercial real estate, construction/land development, business and consumer loans. FFNW demonstrated rolling in a tight range from a support of $12.60 to a ceiling of $13.90 for almost 12 months before breaking out to a recent price point of $19.15.

"Success is more a function of consistent common sense than it is of genius."
– *An Wang*

Maiden Holdings Ltd (MHLD)   Charts by MyRollingStocks.com

Maiden Holdings, Ltd. (Maiden) is a holding company. The company is focused on serving the needs of regional and specialty insurers in the United States, Europe and select other global markets by providing reinsurance solutions designed to support their capital needs. For 13 months, Maiden rolled between $12 support and $13.55 resistance only to breakout upwards to the $17 price range.

"Some people wait so long for their ship to come in, their pier collapses."
– John Goddard

Charter Financial Corporation (CHFN)   Charts by MyRollingStocks.com

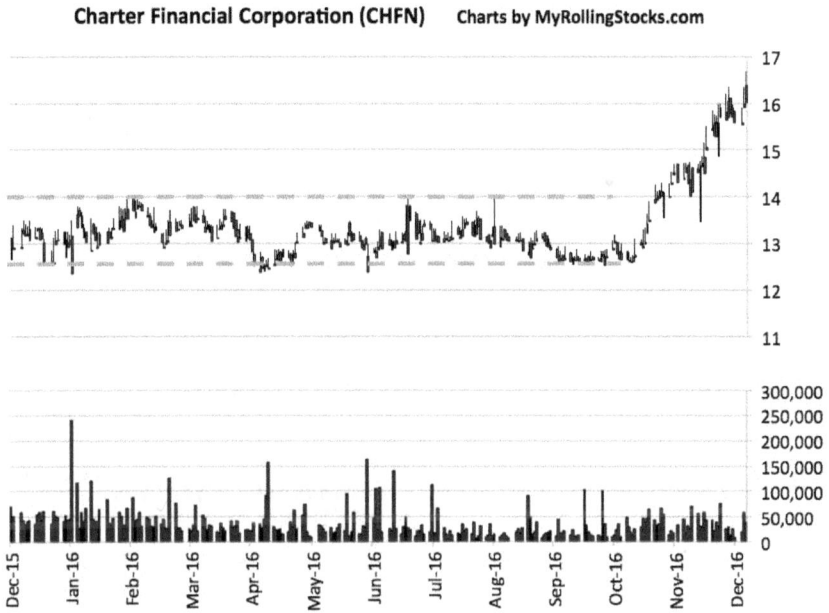

Charter Financial Corporation (CHFN) is a savings and loan holding company for CharterBank (the Bank). The Bank is a federally-chartered savings bank. The Bank's principal business consists of attracting retail deposits from the general public and investing those deposits, together with funds generated from operations, in commercial real estate loans, one- to four-family residential mortgage loans, construction loans and investment securities, commercial business loans, home equity loans and lines of credit, and other consumer loans. CHFN rolled between support and resistance of $12.68 and $13.70, respectively, for 10 months until it broke out to the $16 range in December of 2016.

"I like to buy stocks when the bears are giving them away."
– Warren Buffett

BGC Partners Inc (BGCP)   Charts by MyRollingStocks.com

BGC Partners, Inc. (BGCP) is a global brokerage company servicing the financial and real estate markets. The company operates through two segments: Financial Services and Real Estate Services. BGCP is another example of a rolling stock that broke out of its relatively tight trading range of $8.40 to $9.20 and rose to $10.20 by December of 2016.

CHAPTER 3

The Rolling Stocks Process

Nick Saban's intense focus on process, one could argue, is the main reason for his repeated success as a football coach. Regardless of the school team he coached whether Michigan, Louisiana or Alabama, his process was repeatable, and so are the results. He said, "The process is really what you have to do day in and day out to be successful. We try to define the standard that we want everybody to sort of work toward, adhere to, and do it on a consistent basis. Whatever your endeavor, you can determine the outcome by having a positive attitude, having great work ethic, and having discipline to be able to execute on a consistent basis."

By definition, a process is any repeatable series of steps taken to complete an action. The process that we follow and perform day in and day out to become successful at trading rolling stocks is outlined below. As we describe the process steps, we will provide some insights into the key inputs for each of the process steps. These key inputs are critical to the successful execution of your rolling stocks trading efforts.

THE ROLLING STOCKS PROCESS

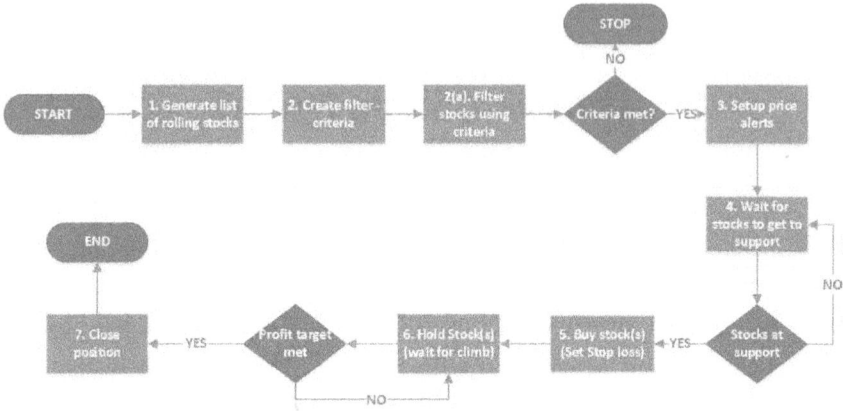

Process Steps

11. Generate the list – How to find rolling stocks

    a. Websites – look at thousands of charts

    b. Online rolling stocks lists – e.g. MyRollingStocks.com

    c. Investing stock group meet-ups

12. Create the filter

    a. Fundamental Analysis (research this)

    b. Volume

    c. PE ratio

13. Set price alerts

14. Patience and Persistence and Market Psychology (Wait,…wait for it)

15. Buying the stocks

    a. Stop loss

"There are one hundred men seeking security to one able man willing to risk his fortune." *– J Paul Getty*

b. Risk management

16. Managing the climb (Patience and Persistence and Market Psychology)

17. Selling the stocks and take profit

Generate the List - How to Find Rolling Stocks

It is not difficult to find these rolling stocks. In fact, you can do it on your own – you just need to know where to look and what to look for. The obvious next question may be what qualifies as a rolling stock? By definition, a rolling stock offers at least three buying opportunities in a 12-month period which will each yield as least a 10% return.

So, let's say you found a rolling stock that you were excited about, and it has been rolling for 12 months between consistent support and resistance levels.

A great source for a rolling stocks list is MyRollingstocks.com (of course) or other similar online sites. A simple Google search for rolling stocks will turn up many sources. Some online brokerage firms also have scanning criteria that you can use to obtain rolling stocks and many other types of patterns. Typically, rolling stocks will be referred to as a rectangular pattern. However, in your travels, you may encounter other stock patterns such as:

- Double Bottom: consisting of two well defined sharp lows at approximately the same price level

- Triple Bottom: consisting of two well defined sharp lows at approximately the same price level

- Head and shoulders bottom: this pattern has the middle of three dips as the lowest – is usually confirmed when the neckline is broken to the top

"The successful speculator must be content, at times, to ignore probably two out of every three apparent opportunities to make money." – *Charles Dow*

- Upside Breakout: this pattern is confirmed when a price closes above a sideways trading range

- Bottom Triangle/wedge: lows and highs forming a triangle with two converging trend lines. A break occurs on the upper trend line.

- Continuation Wedge (bullish): lower lows and lower highs for a downward triangle. A break occurs above the upper trend line

- Symmetrical Continuation Triangle (bullish): when there are lower highs and higher lows, this pattern waits to be confirmed by a breakout above the upper trend line of the triangle

- Ascending Continuation Triangle: As lows are moving increasingly higher, but highs are maintaining a constant price level, this pattern is confirmed by a breach of the upper trend line

- Megaphone Bottom: With the price range continuing to broaden, confirmation of this pattern occurs when a new high is made but a new low is not.

- Flag (bullish): after a steep rise in price, a rectangle channel pattern indicates a pause in the uptrend

- Pennant (bullish): following a steep rise in price, a flag pattern consisting of lower highs and higher lows signal a pause in the uptrend

- Rounded Bottom: the U-shape bottom is confirmed when the price crosses above its moving average

"It isn't as important to buy as cheap as possible as it is to buy at the right time."
– Jesse Livermore

CHAPTER 4

Create the Filter

Warren Buffett once said, "Only buy something that you'd be perfectly happy to hold if the market shut down for 10 years." There are several methods to determine the fair value or the price at which you are comfortable to enter a common stock. As we embark on this journey, there are two main questions that confront us: (1) What is the intrinsic value of the stock? (2) What price is the market willing to pay for the stock? Once you comfortably answer those two questions, you will be ready to slay the proverbial dragon – which is the stock market. Let's tackle the first question - How do you find the intrinsic value of a stock?

You could examine the fundamentals of the company to get an estimate of the intrinsic value of the stock. This analysis will be based on predictions of the future cash flows and profitability of the business. This means that you will compare the market price of the stock to something directly related to its value, such as earnings, book value, sales or cash flow.

Table 2 – Fundamental Analysis (What to buy)
Vs Technical Analysis (When to buy)

Fundamental Analysis	Technical Analysis
Revenue	Advance/Decline ratio
Net Income	Simple Moving Average
Profit margin	Exponential Moving Average
Price earnings ratio	Moving Average Convergence Divergence (MACD)

"If you are considering the purchase of a particular stock but aren't happy with the current price – just wait a minute." – *Market Maxim*

17

Working capital	Stochastic Oscillator
Current ratio	52 week high/low
Debt to Equity	Short interest
Quick ratio	Put/call ratio
Dividend payout ratio	Bollinger bands
Free cash flow	Chandelier exit
PEG ratio	RSI
Return on invested capital (ROIC)	Standard deviation (volatility)
Return on assets (ROA)	Decision Point Price Momentum Oscillator
Price to sales	Pivot points
Market capitalization	Accumulation/Distribution line
Enterprise value (EV)	Ease of Movement (EMV)
EV to Sales	Volume weighted average price (VWAP)
EBITDA	Correlation Coefficient

Price-to-Earnings Ratio

The price-to-earnings ratio (also known as the P/E ratio or earnings multiple) is one of the best-known fundamental ratios, and rightfully so. It's also one of the most valuable. The P/E ratio divides a stock's share price by its earnings per share to come up with a value that represents how much investors are willing to shell out for each dollar of a company's earnings.

The P/E ratio is important because it provides a measuring stick to compare valuations across companies. Another way of putting it, is that a stock with a lower P/E ratio costs less per share for the same level of financial performance than one with a higher P/E. Naturally, an investor would want to pay less for the same return, which essentially means that a P/E ratio is the way to go.

Bear in mind that the P/E ratio should not be compared across different industries. While it's completely reasonable to see a telecom stock such as Verizon or AT&T with a P/E in the teens, a P/E ratio of closer to 30 is perfectly normal in the lodging industry - in fact it's the industry average. As long as apples are compared to apples, the P/E ratio can give an excellent glimpse at a stock's valuation.

When an investor compares the market price of a stock to the earnings per share or book value, he's looking at an evaluation ratio from the perspective of a fundamental analyst. For all purposes, a ratio is just a number to compare to another number. You can track anything with a ratio, right? Let's look at price to earnings ratio.

When we are evaluating a common stock, we compare the price of the stock to the earnings per share to see if a stock is attractively priced. This is called the price to earnings ratio for exactly that reason. The higher the number, the more expensive the stock is. A share of common stock is a share of the company's earnings. The question is, how much are people willing to pay for those earnings? If a stock trades for $25 on the secondary market where the earnings per share is $1, the stock changed by 25 times the earnings or a PE ratio of 25 to 1. This indicates how much investors value a company's profits as expressed through the market price of the stock. In other words, how much are investors willing to pay for a share of the company's profits? Are they willing to pay ten times the earnings, or 20 times the earnings, or 100 times the earnings?

Stocks trading at high multiples are called growth stocks, while those trading at low multiples are called value stocks. Growth stocks tend to be more volatile than value stocks because much of their price is supported by market psychology and enthusiasm rather than the tangible measures such as PE value and other valuation metrics.

Price-to-Book Ratio

The P/E ratio is a good indicator of what investors are paying for each dollar of a company's earnings, and similarly the price-to-book ratio (or P/B ratio) is an equally good indication of what investors are willing to shell out for each dollar of a company's assets. The P/B ratio divides a stock's share price by its net assets, less any intangibles such as goodwill. The P/B is a relatively conservative metric, which could be the reason that it is one of Warren Buffett's favorite metric.

The earnings of a company can be found on the income statement. In a similar fashion, the book value can be determined from the balance sheet. In the event that a company has to be liquidated, the equipment, the factory, the real estate, the machinery would be sold at auction. The creditors would be first in line to collect the proceeds from the auction and next in line would be the preferred stock holders. The amount of money left over, when divided by the shares of common stock, is the book value per share. In other words, this is the hard tangible value of a share of common stock. If the book value of the share of stock is $6 and the stock now trades for $30, then it is trading at a price to book ratio of 5. The book value and the PE ratio helps you to determine if the stock is trading at a high or a low multiple. Stocks that trade at low valuation ratios are called value stocks, while those trading at higher valuation ratios are called growth stocks. Typically, for most stocks, shooting for a P/B of 1.5 or less is a good path to solid value. A low P/B ratio can indicate an undervalued company, however, it can also be a sign of a company in distress.

Debt-Equity

As an investor , you should want to learn more about how a company finances its assets – especially if you're on the prowl for the next big value stock. The debt/equity ratio will be an important tool in your arsenal. As with the P/E ratio, this ratio, which indicates what proportion of financing a company has received from debt (like loans or bonds) and equity (like the issuance of shares of stock), can vary from industry to industry.

Beware of high above-industry debt/equity numbers, especially when an industry is facing difficult times – it could be one of your first signs that a company is getting over its head in debt. You may recall Lehman Brothers, they had a debt/equity ratio of over 30:1 in 2007 before the bankruptcy. That means that for every dollar of equity, the bank had $30 in debt. Be cautious.

Free Cash Flow

Many people are not aware that a company's earnings are rarely equal to the amount of cash it brings in. There is a solid reason for this. Public companies report their financials using GAAP or IFRS accounting principles – or accrual accounting – not the balance of the corporate checking account. While a company could be reporting a huge profit for its latest quarter, the actual cash on hand could be meager.

This is the purpose of free cash flow - it tells an investor how much actual cash a company is left with after any capital investments. As an investor, you want companies that have positive free cash flow. This metric, along with the debt-equity ratio, is more significant during difficult economic times.

PEG Ratio

The price/earnings to growth ratio (or PEG ratio) is a modified version of the P/E ratio that also takes earnings growth into account. One way to find stocks of companies that are undervalued and growing is by looking at their PEG ratios. It is highly likely that these companies may gain positive attention in upcoming quarters. Like the P/E ratio, this metric varies from industry to industry.

In some cases, especially for young growth companies, these companies may have no earnings or profits. If the company has no earnings, it really isn't worth talking about a PE ratio. In such a case, you will see "not applicable." In these cases, it is more prudent to compare a market price of the stock to the sales the company makes. We can, therefore, research some other metrics, such as price to sales and price to cash ratios.

"I'd be a bum on the street with a tin cup if the markets were always efficient."
– *Warren Buffett*

You may notice that these metrics tie in closely with the income statement. Earnings represent the bottom line, while sales represent the top line. If a company is not making a profit, you can compare the price of the stock to the cash flow generated per share. This is called price per cash.

As an investor, you need a healthy dose of skepticism, because many companies have demonstrated that it's very easy to manipulate earnings with some creative accounting. The sales to revenue ratio is a very hard number to manipulate. It is the top line of the income statement, and it hasn't been filtered through all the subtractions of cost of goods sold, operating expenses, depreciation, amortization or interest.

Let's talk briefly about market capitalization. A company's market capitalization (often times abbreviated as market cap) is their total number of upstanding shares multiplied by today's closing price. It is that simple. Market capitalization is simply the total value of all of upstanding shares. If a company has a market capitalization of under one billion dollars, it is usually considered small cap. For example, let's say that a company has 10 million shares upstanding and the shares close at $25 today - the market capitalization is simply 250 million. Since that is under one billion, that makes it a small cap stock. Companies that have a market cap up to $10 billion are considered mid cap, while those above that are considered large cap. In today's environment, the Facebooks, IBMs, Microsofts, GEs, Apples and the Googles of the world are large caps.

Technical Analysis

Whereas fundamental analysts examine a company's intrinsic value, technical analysts, on the other hand, study the behavior of the stock as it trades in the market. Technical analysts do not care much about a company's product, how it's been selling, how effective the new CEO or management should be or could be. They want to know how the shares of the company stock have been trading in terms of the market price and the volume levels. Technical analysts study stock market data. They look at charts and patterns.

Speaking of charts and patterns, technical chartists believe, in terms of stock prices, that history tends to repeat itself. Many technical traders make decisions on whether to buy or sell by looking at charts or a stock market's price over a certain time period. These traders may view price patterns over 200 days, 30 days, 5 days or even 1 day. The idea is that by watching the stock pattern, these traders will see trends develop. The trader uses these charts to determine the direction of stock prices over the near term.

There are some popular chart types. In fact, rolling stocks is one such chart type. With rolling stocks, we are simply looking at resistance and support price points. We are looking at how a company's stock price might be trending over a period of time. We typically combine some technical analysis with some fundamental analysis as a basis for entering the trade. The rolling stock method supports the idea that you will choose a stock that is fundamentally sound that also happens to be a rolling stock.

Technical Signals

This might be a great time to mention a few of the more common technical signals that we have employed over the years. The proper use of these technical signals has had a positive effect on our portfolio. They have helped us to determine the right entry price point for stocks. There are three main indicators we have used over the years. They are the simple moving average, the moving average convergence divergence (MACD) and the stochastics indicators.

Moving Averages

You may think of the moving average as a tool to smooth out stock prices. Typically, stock prices have a lot of random variation or "noise" – when the moving average is applied to these prices, it has a smoothing or filtering

"Opportunity is a moving target, and the bigger the opportunity, the faster it moves."
- Richard Gaylord Briley

effect. Because it is based on past prices, the moving average (MA) is a lagging indicator. There are different variations of the moving average. The simple moving average (SMA) is the simple arithmetic average of a stock's price over a defined time period. The exponential moving average (EMA) is a weighted average and gives a larger weight to a more recent stock price. Moving averages play a critical role when determining the optimal price points for buying rolling stocks. They are commonly used to determine support and resistance levels. Moving averages are like building blocks; they form the basis for other indicators such as the Moving Average Convergence Divergence (MACD), which is a key input when analyzing rolling stocks.

Moving Average Convergence Divergence (MACD)

The MACD is a trend-following momentum indicator that shows the relationship between two moving averages of prices. If you were so inclined to actually calculate the MACD signal line, you would need to take the difference between the two EMAs. This difference would result in a nine-day moving average. This calculation can be a laborious undertaking. That's why there are now many sophisticated charting software programs, which make life easy with back-testing capabilities that automatically prepare all the calculations instantly for you.

The popularity of the MACD is largely due to its ability to help quickly spot increasing short-term momentum. We will not go into the inner working of the MACD (a quick Google search can fill that gap).

The main thing to know is that when the MACD falls below the signal line, it is a bearish signal, and you should consider selling. Conversely, when the MACD rises above the signal line, the indicator gives a bullish signal, suggesting that the price of the stock is likely to increase.

The **Stochastic Oscillator** is our third and most favored technical indicator. Any charting software worth its weight will have an option to add these technical signals to the charts. The Stochastic oscillator is a leading indicator that measures the relationship between a stock's closing price and its price range over a predetermined period of time. We use the stochastic oscillator to determine when a stock has moved into an overbought or oversold position. The stochastics is a favorite technical indicator because of its high degree of accuracy. Since this is our favorite indicator, it serves that we will bore you with the gory details of its conceptual origins.

The premise of the stochastics indicator holds that a stock's closing price tends to trade at the high end of the day's price action. Price action is the price at which a stock traded throughout the daily session. The stock may have opened at $10.00, traded as low as $9.75 and as high as $10.75, and closed at $10.50 for the day. The price action of this example is between $9.75 (the low of the day) and $10.75 (the high of the day). If the stock, however, is currently in a downtrend cycle, the closing prices will tend to close at or near the low end of the price action. The indicator is generated by looking at the difference between the current closing price and the lowest low for several trading periods compared to the difference between the highest high and the lowest low for the same number of trading periods.

With this indicator, there are two lines. The indicator chart typically has lines drawn at both the "20" and "80" values as warning signals. Values exceeding "80" are interpreted as a strong overbought condition, or "selling" signal. If the curve dips below "20", a strong oversold condition, or "buying" signal, is generated.

Relative Strength Index (RSI): This is a momentum oscillator that measures the speed and change of price movements. RSI oscillates between 0 and 100. When reading the RSI, a stock is considered overbought when the RSI is above 70 and oversold when it is below 30. Signals can also be generated by looking for divergences, failure swings and centerline crossovers. RSI can also be used to identify the general trend.

"No one can achieve real and lasting success or get rich in business by being a conformist." – *J Paul Getty*

CHAPTER 5

Setting Price Alerts & Buying the Stocks

Any online brokerage firm that is worth your time and money will have tools that can be used to set price alerts. If your online brokerage firm does not have these tools, then either it's time to find a new brokerage house or you may search to find some tools online. Nasdaq.com has a cool price alert tool. Once you create an account at Nasdaq.com, the custom stock alerts tool automatically sends you e-mails when the stocks you've entered match your pre-set conditions in the pre-market, regular hours or after-hours trading sessions. If your interest in alerts is limited to rolling stocks, then myrollingstocks.com offers price alerts, albeit those alerts are limited to rolling stocks.

Regardless of the tool or alert service you use, the alerts window should have a conditions area where you define the conditions which must be met to activate the alert. You should be able to create alerts based on price movement, time and date, trading volume or the state of your margin cushion. Alert actions include sending a notification such as a pop-up message on your trading screen, an email or a text message, or initiating an order, specifically a buy or sell order.

Buying the Stocks

So you were just notified via an alert that a stock on your list has entered your buy range. What now? Once you get an alert, you should carefully observe the stock and place your buy order at your predetermined support price. We recommend that you buy these rolling stocks on a day order and set your entry price at the mid-point between the ask and the bid price. In the majority of cases, my order is filled by the end of the day. In the rare cases when the order is not filled, I will review my criteria and reevaluate the stock before the next trading session.

Sometimes exercising patience is the most difficult thing to learn. I remember back in college when I was on the varsity track team, and I was very late to practice one day because of this girl I wanted to see. When I finally showed up at track practice, coach pulled me aside and said, "Son, she will be there when you are done with practice – there is no need to chase her." A similar piece of advice can be applied to stocks, you do not need to chase them and if the price is not right, you do not need to keep changing your orders to get your order filled. Do not let your emotions get the better of you and chase a stock up the pole. Remember to always keep your cool.

We also recommend that you look to purchase rolling stocks that have daily volume of approximately 100,000 shares. This does not mean that you should completely rule out a rolling stock that has a daily volume of 50,000 shares. It means that this stock will require more analysis and due diligence before you pull the trigger.

 For stocks that have low average volume, a general rule of thumb is to never buy more than 5% of a stock's average daily volume. For example, if a stock has an average daily volume of 50,000 shares, you should never buy more than 2,500 shares.

Exercising Patience

The hardest thing to do when faced with either a potential stock that was not filled at your price target, or when faced with mounting losses on a stock that you own, is to remain cool and be confident. When you learn to control your fear and have confidence both in yourself and in your trading

"If you have to go through too much investigation, then something is wrong."
- Warren Buffett

strategy, you will make trading profits. Just remember that patience and persistence lead to potential profits.

I remember the first time I started trading stocks - the adrenaline rush was overwhelming. I bought a stock at what I considered a fair price and, as is the case with most individual investors, I expected the stock to go up. However, as soon as I bought it, it started tanking. It went down like a brick, and I panicked and sold at the bottom. Do you know that feeling you get when you are climbing the drop tower ride at the amusement park? You know the thrill is coming, but you are not sure just when you will get to the top and start the sudden and sharp fall. As soon as I bought the stock and it went south, I experienced the sweaty palms, my heart was racing and my pulse was so loud it drowned out the traffic and beeping horns on the busy street below. My mouth felt as dry as a desert even though I just drank a glass of water. My emotions were swirling - what happened if I lost money – how would I explain it to my family, to myself? It was a remarkable feeling – I paced back and forth, I went for long walks and tried to get back to the point where it all went south and think back to what if and why and all the things I could have or should have done. How do you get out of your head and learn to control that fear? How do you become confident – but not over-confident or cocky? Do you recall that I said I panicked and sold the stock? Well …a few weeks later the stock was 8% higher than where I had originally bought it.

It takes time and practice to overcome or control the fear of losing money. While you may never completely overcome it, the fear itself should never drive your decisions. One of my finance professors once said money only buys you time and convenience. My method to overcome the fear, which will be different from yours, is to remind myself of that fact. And to quote Ayn Rand, "Money is only a tool. It will take you wherever you wish, but it will not replace you as the driver." The bottom line, and the most important point of this chapter, is that you should never allow your fear to be the driving force for your decisions.

"If you can count your money, then you don't have a billion dollars." – *J Paul Getty*

Market Psychology - the Crowd Effect

The market is made up of professional traders as well as individual investors like you and me. The collective fear of these individuals is the market's psychology. While there are some quants and high frequency traders who use computer driven algorithms to mitigate the human emotional element of trading, this has not altered the overall psychology of the market in the aggregate.

Market psychology is one of the many factors that drive stock prices. There are many people – just like us – who are making decisions based on the information that is available to them. In his 1967 provocative and entertaining bestseller, *The Money Game*, journalist George A.W. Goodman argued that "In the long run, future earnings represent present value, but in the short run the dominant factor is the elusive *Australopithecus*, the temper of the crowd."

In Justin Fox's book *The Myth of the Rational Market*, the author is not a strong proponent of the wisdom of crowds. Crowds and markets possess many useful traits, but wisdom is not one of them, he says. "When men are brought together, they no longer decide by chance and independently of each other, but react upon one another," reads a thought of Henri Poincaré quoted in the book. "Many causes come into action, they trouble the men and draw them this way and that, but there is one thing they cannot destroy, the habits they have of Panurge's sheep." The reference to Panurge describes an individual who blindly follows others regardless of the consequences.

Later in the same book, *The Myth of the Rational Market*, author Justin Fox notes, "Stock prices contain lots of information." He later paraphrases Friedrich Hayek: "Markets are the best aggregators of information known to man, yet mixed up amid the information in security prices is an awful lot of emotion, error, and noise."

"Courage is doing what you are afraid to do. There can be no courage unless you are scared." – *Eddie Rickenbacker*

Treat it Like a Business

You must treat your trading endeavor like a business. This is true whether you have $1,000 or $100,000 in your trading portfolio. You will, of course, make your investment decisions carefully with sufficient fundamental analysis and careful attention to the stock's technical attributes. You must remember Warren Buffett's two rules. Rule number one is to never lose money and rule number two is to never forget rule number one. You must think of yourself as the money manager. The success of your enterprise will depend on your decision-making skills, your ability to manage risk, and on whether you invest in the right tools and resources to make your organization successful.

Once you make a decision to buy a stock, you are effectively buying a business. The next step is to manage that business with the same zeal and gravitas that you used when performing your initial analysis and due diligence. After buying the stock, your expectation is that the stock will go up. However, in some cases the stock may also go down after you buy it. You have no control over the stock price, and you have no control over the news or other factors that may significantly affect the stock's price. These are the factors that you need to be aware of and manage accordingly. I monitor my positions constantly (I average 7 times per day, however, you may not need to check your positions as often as I do), but you need to be aware of where you are in the market. Since we all have information readily available at our finger tips, there is no excuse for not knowing where your positions are during the trading session.

Stop Losses

The use of stop loss is a reaction to your own emotional response to losses. A stop-loss order is an order you give to your broker to exit a trade if it goes against you by some amount. For a buyer, the stop-loss order is a sell order.

From a risk management perspective, we suggest that you enter your stop-loss order at the same time you enter your buy position. Based on risk management rules, you need to know the stop in order to calculate how big a position to take in the first place.

Some stop loss rules are fixed while others are self-adjusting. You need to choose the type of stop that works best for you. Stops typically relate to technical indicators, money, or time, and there is no magic formula that will tell you which ones are best for each situation. We will describe a few below, but there are others that you may need to research on your own.

Stop orders are not triggered by the bid/ask but rather by the last sale. Let's say you find a rolling stock that you like (preferably from myrollingstocks.com) and the stock is trading between $21 and $23. For some reason, you decide that this stock may break out and go higher, so you place a buy stop above the current market price. A buy stop placed at $23 means that the stock has to reach $23 or higher for the order to be filled. Once the price gets to $23 and is triggered – it becomes a market order.

In another scenario, let's say you have a rolling stock in your portfolio that has been doing well for you. You bought it at $17, and it's currently trading at $37. You determine that the stock is hitting up against resistance at this $37 price point. You would enter a sell stop at $36. This means that if the stock stays above $37, then you will stay in it. However, don't get greedy. You can use a sell stop to lock in your gains.

The 7-8 Percent Stop Loss Rule

The 7-8 percent rule states that you should stop a loss when it reaches 7-8 percent of the starting equity. The 7-8 percent rule is an example of a money stop, which names the amount of money you're willing to lose in a single trade. The 7- 8 percent stop-loss rule refers to cutting losses when the stock price falls 7-8 percent below the purchase price. Commission costs are not included. This rule was set specifically at 7-8 percent because

"Successful investing is anticipating the anticipation of others."
- John Maynard Keynes

our research shows that successful stocks rarely fall in price more than 7 or 8 percent below a proper buy point. If you buy stocks at the pivot point, you may want to cut your losses even sooner. 8 percent is considered a maximum stop loss.

Risk Reward Money Stops

This is the ratio of the expected gain to the expected loss. The higher the risk-reward ratio is, the more desirable the trade will be. Say, for example, that you're buying XYZ stock at $10, and your indicators tell you that the potential gain is $20, which means that the stock could go to $30. If you set your initial stop at $5 (50 percent of your capital stake) for the chance to make $20, that gives you a risk-reward ratio of 20:5 or 4:1.

Maximum Adverse Excursion (MAE)

The concept of maximum adverse excursion (MAE) was developed by John Sweeney. This concept is the statistically determined worst-case loss that may occur during the course of your trade. This is actually quite useful in a rolling stock scenario. You would calculate the biggest change in the high-low range over a fixed period (it could be 3 months or the length of period of one roll) that's equivalent to your usual holding period. Let's go back to the WFM example. The stock was rolling between $28.00 and $34.00. If your entry point is $28.00, the maximum range is $6.00 and hence your stop loss would be set at $6.00.

Trailing Stops

Trailing stops follow the price of the stock; the level of the stop increases as the trade makes profits. The trailing stop is set on a money basis. For example, if you enter the stock at $28 and the current stock price is now at

$34, you could say that you want to keep 80 percent of the gain. You'd raise the stop every day to include 80 percent of the day's gain.

Time Stops

Sometimes you have money tied up in a trade that is going nowhere sideways. You recognize that that money could be put to better use in a different trade. A time stop can be used to exit the trade and find a different security that is moving.

Limit Order

Sometimes I like to name my own price, and I am sure that, at some point, you will want to name your own price as well. If the stock is at $67, maybe you are interested in selling it at $69 – you would enter a sell limit order above the current market price. A sell limit of $69 suggests that you want a price of $69 or better for your stock. If the bid rises to $69 or even $69.05, your limit order will be executed and you will sell your stock.

Let's say there is a stock currently trading at $24 and you are interested in buying the stock at $21. You would place a buy limit order below the current price. This means you will only buy the stock if you can get it for $21 or less. If the stock never gets to your price, your order would not be filled, and you would not buy the stock.

Stop-Limit Order

We can get even fancier and talk about a stop limit order. I do not personally use a stop-limit order, but for whatever reason, some people may like them. In this case, your order specifies the most you are willing to pay for the stock or the least that you will accept for a stock that you already own. For example – if you own a rolling stock that is now trading at $45 and it has done really well for you, a sell stop limit at $45 would be triggered only

"We make a living by what we get, but we make life by what we give."
- Winston Churchill

if the stock hits $45 or lower. However, you are saying that you will not take less than $45 per share for this stock. So, the order may get triggered and the bid falls to $44.85, in which case you will be holding on to this stock for a while – because the sell order would not execute.

A buy stop limit at $23 would start out just like a buy stop order. The stock has to hit $23 or higher before it gets triggered. However, by adding the limit order into the mix, you are saying you will not pay more than $23 for the stock.

Advanced Order Types - One Cancels Other

A One-Cancels-Other order (OCO) is a conditional order. Conditional orders are orders that can be submitted or cancelled based on some prede-termined criteria. An OCO order is a fancy way to enter two orders at once to help you manage your orders more efficiently. This is a pair of orders which states that if one order is executed, then the other order is automati-cally canceled. It combines a stop order with a limit order on an automated trading platform. When either the stop or limit level is reached and the order executed, the other order will be automatically canceled.

Let's review an example of where you might use an OCO order. If you own 1,000 shares of a rolling stock that is currently trading at $12 and the stock has been rolling between a support of $11 and $14 resistance. You expect the stock to continue in this range for the next several months. From a risk management perspective (using the Maximum Adverse Excursion), you would like to lose no more than $3 on the stock. You can place an OCO order, which would consist of a stop-loss order to sell 1,000 shares at $8, and a simultaneous limit order to sell 1,000 shares at $14, whichever occurs first. These orders could either be day orders or good-till-canceled orders.

If and when the stock trades up to $14, the limit order to sell would be exe-cuted, and your holding of 1,000 shares would be sold at $14. At the same time, the $8 stop-loss order will be automatically canceled.

One Triggers Other

A One Triggers Other (OTO) order is also a conditional order that allows you to enter an initial order and place a second order contingent upon the fill of the first order. This type of order is especially powerful when trading rolling stocks.

We will use the same example as before with the rolling stock that is trading between a support of $11 and a resistance of $14. As an order entry process, you could place an OTO order to place a limit order to buy the stock at $11 and then place a sell stop order that will be automatically entered upon the execution of the initial buy order.

One Triggers Two Orders

The one-triggers-two order type is a conditional order that is also very well suited to rolling stocks. The one-triggers-two order type goes one step further than the one-cancels-other order type. The one-triggers-two order-entry system allows you to enter a primary order and place two secondary (OCO) orders. These secondary (OCO) orders will be active only upon the complete fill of the primary order. Please note that a partial fill of the primary order will not trigger the OCO. When one of the secondary orders executes, the other will cancel immediately.

So what does this mean for you? Let's outline and review a quick example in the table below.

Example for One Triggers Two Order Type

Stock Symbol	WFM
Support	$28.10
Resistance	$34.00
Stop Loss (Using 7% stop loss rule)	$26.04
Stop Loss (Using MAE rule)	$22.00

"When you reach for the stars, you may not get one, but you won't come up with a handful of mud either." – Leo Burnett

To execute the One-Triggers-Two, we would do the following steps:

1. Enter an opening primary limit order to buy WFM at $28.10

2. Enter the first of the two secondary orders. Enter a sell stop order to sell WFM. In our example, this order is a sell stop. We are going to sell WFM at $26.04 – this means that if the stock slips below $26.04 the stock will be sold.

3. Enter the second of the two secondary orders. We will enter to sell WFM with a limit price of $33.50. A sell limit of $33.50 means that we will sell if we can get a price of $33.50 or better.

In the mini case study above, if we had decided to use the MAE rule for the stop loss in step two above, we would have entered the sell stop order at $22.00 instead of $26.04. The specific steps may vary depending of the broker you use. You may need to check with your brokerage firm to understand how to structure the trade on their trading platform.

CHAPTER 6

Managing Risk

Stocks may experience significant price changes in a short time period due to changing investor demand in the marketplace. Consequently, volatility is one of the greatest risks you will face when you invest in stocks. When you invest in rolling stocks, you are aiming to get into a stock at the support price level. However, you may not always be correct in your assessment and there will be times when the stock you thought was at the support price may keep falling. This may occur because of disappointing earnings or some other news event. For example, you may have bought a stock for $15 a share and it dropped $3 in price in the following week because of disappointing news about a new product. In this case, you suffered a 20 percent loss. If you had purchased 200 shares at a cost of $3,000, your investment would now be worth just $2,400. You would have lost $600, plus whatever transaction fees you paid. Of course, this is a fictitious example and should not happen to you because of the stringent stop loss rules that you employ.

Each investor will have a different risk profile. While some investors may prefer to go for the big prize and hence take on more risk, we believe it is prudent to minimize risk and realize a satisfactory return. If that's your approach, you might consider some basic investment strategies: asset allocation, diversification, rebalancing and focusing on the trend.

"You want 21% risk free? Pay off your credit cards." – *Andrew Tobias*

Asset Allocation

Allocating your assets means that you are deciding —usually on a percentage basis—what portion of your total portfolio to invest in different asset classes, such as stocks, bonds, and cash or cash equivalents. If you are trying to minimize risk, you should have all your money in one asset class. Let's say you are 42 and you have 58% of your assets in stocks – that 58% in stocks should also be diversified.

Asset allocation is a useful tool in managing systematic risk because different categories of investments respond to changing economic and political conditions in different ways (that is so true especially in today's political climate). By including different asset classes in your portfolio, you increase the likelihood that some of your investments will provide satisfactory returns even if others are fall flat.

Using Diversification

Essentially, diversification means – do not put all your financial eggs in one basket. It is best to choose a mix of different types of investments, which is called diversification. When you diversify, it's important to divide the money you've allocated not only into different asset classes, but also within those particular asset classes. Just as in the previous example, let's say you are 42 years old and you have 58% of your assets in stocks. Within the stock category, you might choose subclasses based on different market capitalizations and different sectors of the economy.

When you generate your list of rolling stocks and the stock price alert starts flashing on your radar, you should have already performed the due diligence and fundamental analysis on each company so that you know their market capitalization and market sector. Using the rolling stocks strategy does not preclude you from performing the basic fundamental analysis. That would be like saying – now that I am a race car driver, I do not need to obey traffic signals. Hello! I do not think we need to explain the importance of obeying the traffic signals.

With any investment strategy, especially with rolling stocks, asset allocation and diversification are undoubtedly important – but it is equally important that you stay actively attuned to the results of your choices.

Rebalancing

Whenever we have a conversation about investing, this term of 'rebalancing' is typically a frequent reference. What does it mean? It means that at some point in time your portfolio was balanced and it should now be re-balanced. It also means that you should only allocate anywhere from five percent (5%) to seven percent (7%) of your portfolio to any one stock.

Let's say, for example, that you have $100,000 to invest in stocks, and you could allocate anywhere from $5,000 to $7,000 to each stock purchase. If the market suddenly takes off (maybe because a real estate tycoon wins the US electoral college contest), you may find a large number of current assets held within one stock. For example, let's say you had GE and MSFT in your portfolio, if MSFT increased in value by 25% while GE only increased by 3%. What should you do in such a scenario? You should sell some of MSFT and maybe buy a different stock or hold cash. The rebalancing act allows you to redirect some of the funds other investments. By having funds spread out across multiple stocks, a downturn in one will be partially offset by the activities of the others, which can provide a level of portfolio stability.

Follow the Trend

Do you recall the old market axiom, "The trend is your friend until it ends?" One way to manage investment risk is to commit to only buying stocks that are in an uptrend and to sell them once they violate their trend line support. This is especially true for rolling stocks. When you review the case studies chapter later on in this book, you will see the support and resistance lines we have drawn. You can also draw your own trend lines by connecting a series of higher lows on a chart. If the price breaks the support level by a predetermined amount, you sell.

Summary

Managing risk is about the allocation and diversification of holdings in your portfolio. It is imperative that when you choose new stocks to add to your portfolio, you are keenly aware of what you already own and how the new investment will help you to achieve greater balance. For example, you might include some investments that may be volatile because they have the potential to increase dramatically in value, which other investments in your portfolio are unlikely to do.

Several years ago, economists Harry Markowitz, William Sharpe and Merton Miller shared the Nobel Prize in 1990 for their work on balancing risk and reward by looking for investments that are not correlated with each other. Believe it or not, if you approach risk as we outlined above, you're being influenced by what's called modern portfolio theory, or sometimes simply portfolio theory. Even though it is considered standard practice today, the concept of minimizing risk by combining volatile and price-stable investments in a single portfolio was not a common investing practice as recent as several years ago. Thank goodness that we are smarter about managing risk now than we were several years ago.

"Even if you are on the right track, you will get run over if you just sit there."
- Will Rogers

CHAPTER 7

Introduction to Options

Before we talk about one of the most powerful, yet conservative, trading strategies that you have probably heard of, let's discuss options. Options are derivatives – they are not so difficult to understand once you understand the basic concepts.

Let's use a very simple but brief story to explain the concept of options.

A guy, let's call him Mr. Cocky Guy, walks into a Starbucks coffee shop with a large Dunkin Donuts cup of coffee. He glances around the shop and he strolls over to the newspaper stand. He picks up a newspaper and casually walks over to one of the long communal tables (these are now common in many Starbucks coffee shops).

He makes a beeline for an open chair which just happens to be next to a cute looking blonde and directly across from a dude who looks too old to be her boyfriend (but these days you never know). As he sits down and takes a long casual and noncommittal look at the newspaper, his phone rings. He puts the phone to his ear and his expression softens as he hears a familiar voice on the other end.

"I am sitting at a Starbucks coffee house," he tells the person on the other end of the phone. "I came here to try their coffee but, I had to drive past my Dunkin Donuts shop along the way and I just could not resist, so I stopped and got a cup of Dunkin Donuts coffee. " He continues his phone banter for a few more seconds and then he exclaimed,

"Well, it's not just their coffee, I don't like their stock either. I will bet you that it's headed for the dumpster, just like these used coffee grounds they have here in these bins."

He notices the blond and the guy looking at him and he decides to go in for the kill,

"As far as I am concerned," he pauses, glances at the blond and says just loud enough for them to hear, "Starbucks is for yoga-loving, left-leaning, pretentious people who all received participation trophies and undeserved grades in school to protect their feelings."

"Why don't you tell us all how you really feel," muttered one of the young twenty-something baristas.

The blond glances at him quizzically, and with a wry smile she says, "Well that is a bold and judgmental statement."

"I speak my mind freely and this is the era of Trump, so I call them as I see them. And," he continues to string his bait, "as a matter of fact, I will bet anyone in this coffee shop that Starbucks shares will not go above $60 for the rest of the year."

"Well then – I will take that bet," says the friend. In less than 7 minutes, there were seven or eight people lined up to take the bet from Mr. Cocky Guy. They were all betting that, without a doubt, Starbucks common stock (SBUX) would rise above $60 a share at some point between today (September 1) and the rest of the year.

To make all these bets, the guy had to be creative. He went and gathered a handful of napkins from the condiments bar and wrote the following:

- Buy 100 Shares STARBUCKS at $60 each – Good thru 3rd Friday in December

Anyone in the coffee shop that morning who took the bet and thought that Starbucks stock would rise above $60 per share had to pay the guy $400.

"A person is born with a liking for profit."
– Xunzi c.312 BC-c.230 BC, Chinese Confucian philosopher

The guy ended up collecting $400 each from 10 customers and walked away with $4000 in premiums.

As the guy walks away from the Starbucks, he is elated for about one minute. Then the reality hits him – he collected $4000 from these people (who are all betting that the stock will rise above $60). What if he is wrong and the stock rises to $70 before the end of the year? What would that mean to him? He would have to buy the stock at $70 per share and deliver it to these ten people at $60 per share. He started to feel sweaty and nauseous, so he sat down once again and broke out another napkin to map out this scenario.

If SBUX goes to $70 …before the 3rd Friday in December of this year, he would have to do the following:

- Purchase SBUX $70 per share

- Purchase 1000 share …..$70,000 (There were 10 people -who each bet 100 shares)

- Sell SBUX for $60 share

- Sell 1000 shares of SBUX for $60,000

- In the hole for $10,000

- Premium collected $4000

- Actual loss $6000

This was the napkin scribble for one scenario. What is his actual risk? His risk is unlimited. If SBUX goes to $300 between today and the 3rd Friday in December, this guy would have to buy SBUX for $60 per share and sell it for $300 per share to the holder of the napkin option.

What if SBUX never goes above $60 per share over the next 4 months? No one will ever call him and demand to buy the stock for $60 per (which is what this guy is hoping).

"Fortune is like the market, where, many times, if you can stay a little, the price will fall." – *Francis Bacon (1561-1626, English philosopher, statesman, scientist, jurist and author)*

To explain the concept – this guy actually sold a call option – he sold the Starbucks (SBUX) December $60 call option @$4. How did I get $4? Each person paid him $400 for 100 shares. Each option contract controls 100 share of stock. As the writer of the option, he granted any buyer, who was willing to pay $400, the right to buy 100 shares of Starbucks common stock for $60 per share anytime between today and the end of the contract period.

If you happen to be one of the lucky ones who bought one of those contracts, when would you want to use or exercise it? I suppose if Starbucks rose above $60 per share. In fact, since you paid $4.00 for the right to buy Starbucks at $60, Starbucks would have to rise to $64 – your breakeven point – before it would become worthwhile to exercise your option.

In any event, Mr. Cocky Guy who wrote/sold the calls gets the $4000 in premiums. If Starbucks never gets above $60 by the third Friday in December, he will be smiling all the way to the bank.

It is easier to think of a call option as a bet between a buyer and a seller. The buyer thinks the price of the underlying commodity or thing is going up, and the seller disagrees. Of course, they could settle their disagreements in multiple ways – but they choose to settle it by putting up some money.

The buyer pays the seller a **premium**. Because he puts down some money, he gets the right to buy 100 shares of a particular stock for a set price within a defined time frame.

The buyer pays a **premium** and receives the right to buy a particular stock at a set price (**the strike price or exercise price**) within a defined time frame. The end of that time frame is called **the expiration date**.

Call Options

As we illustrated with Mr. Cocky Guy, a Facebook (FB) Dec 130 call gives the call buyer the right to buy FB common stock for $130 at any time up to the expiration date in December (the third Friday in December). If the stock goes up to $150 before the expiration date, then the owner of the call could still buy the stock for $130. So what happens if the stock suddenly went to $300? The owner of the call option could still buy the stock at $130.

Call option owners are betting that the stocks will go up and beyond the **strike price**. In the case of the FB option mentioned above, the strike price is $130. Just imagine that you bought a stock for $130 and it went up to $300 - you would be ecstatic and so would I.

For call options when the price of the stock trades above the strike price, the option is said to be **in-the-money.** A FB Dec $130 call would begin to trade in-the-money as soon as FB began to trade above $$130 per share.

Time and Intrinsic Value

Let's get a little bit deeper into options. An option can possess two types of values: intrinsic value and time value. For call options, the intrinsic value is the difference between the strike price and the stock price (it is another way of saying how much higher the stock price is compared to the strike price). For example, if our FB stock is trading at $130, how far in the money is the Sept $120 call option. If you said $10, then you were obviously paying attention to the earlier parts of this chapter. The stock price is above the strike price by $10; therefore, the call has an intrinsic value of $10.

Now, what happens if the stock is trading out of the money? If FB is trading at $115, the Sept $120 call would have no intrinsic value. If you were to pay a premium for this out-of-the money call option, it would be because there is sufficient time left for the price to improve or increase. If this is May, then the option does not expire for another 4 months, some brave souls could decide that the stock could climb by $5 in that time period. In this case, there is a **time value** attached to the option. Time value is simply that the option could become more valuable given the amount of time left to expiration.

"The alchemists in their search for gold discovered many other things of greater value."
- *Arthur Schopenhauer (1788-1860, German philosopher and writer)*

If you were to look up the definition of time value of an option, you might find the following definition: An option's time value is equal to its premium (the cost of the option) minus its intrinsic value (the difference between the strike price and the price of the underlying). If the FB call option we mentioned earlier was at-the-money or out-of-the-money, the premium represents time value. Whenever an option is in-the-money, the time value is the difference between the intrinsic value and the premium.

If our FB stock is trading at $115 and the Sept $110 calls are selling for $7, then the call is in the money by $5. However, a trader had to pay a premium of $7. Why the difference? If the call is in the money by $5, why would the trader pay $7? Where is the additional $2 coming from? This is where the time value comes in. If there is still time left for the stock to perform, some people will gladly pay the extra $2.

Exercise Trade Expire

There are a few other important details that we should learn about options. Options can be bought and sold just like stocks. Some of the terms you will see with regard to options are "opening", "closing", and "exercising".

Let's say Mr. Cocky Guy saw that FB was trading at $115 and had reason to believe that FB was going to $130 in the next two weeks. He wants to buy 10 FB contracts with a $130 strike price. When he logs into his online broker, he would enter an order to "**buy to open**" 10 contracts of the Oct $130 call. Now, you need to remember that each contract controls 100 shares. So when Mr. Cocky Guy saw that the quote was $3.10 for the FB Oct $130 call – he knew immediately that each contract was going cost him $310 and, hence, 10 contracts would cost him $3100.

Mr. Cocky Guy got really lucky, and FB shot up to $135 in two weeks. When he logged into his online brokerage account, he saw that each contract was now worth $8.75 – he was flabbergasted and almost too excited to act. Anyway, he was able to gather his wits and enter a trade to close the position. He entered an order to "**sell to close**" all 10 contracts. He just made $5650 in less than two weeks. He could finally afford to be cocky.

Mr. Cocky Guy decided to trade the options for their intrinsic value. However, he could have chosen to **exercise** the option. In that case, he would buy the stock at the strike price and then sell it at the current market price. The smart money usually avoids exercising the option – since it makes more sense to trade the option for its intrinsic value.

There is one other scenario that we have not yet spoken about. Mr. Cocky Guy is not going to enjoy this scenario as much as he did the previous scenarios. In this hypothetical case, FB stock dropped from $115 to $80 in two weeks and traded in a narrow channel for the next month. When Mr. Cocky Guy logged into his account, he saw the value of his option was hovering around $0.05. Over the next month, the option eventually went to $0. In this case, he allowed the options to **expire** worthless.

Put Options

Since we are talking about options, we might as well mention put options. A put option gives the owner the right to sell the stock at a predetermined price. In our previous example, if Mr. Cocky Guy bought the FB Oct $100 put option, he would have the right to sell the stock for $100 even though the stock may have dropped to $80. Heck, even if the FB stock had dropped as low as $15, Mr. Cocky Guy would still have been able to sell the stock for $80. That is how puts work – it's a beautiful thing. Why would you buy a put? If you think a stock has the potential to drop in price – then you would buy a put option. This may be difficult to believe but as the stock price drops below the strike price, the value of the put option increases.

If you had a stock in your portfolio that was trading at $15, wouldn't you like to sell that to someone for $45. That is exactly what a put option allows you to do. If you wanted to exercise the put, you could just buy the stock for

$15 and turn around and sell it immediately for $45. However, as we saw with call options, the smart money does not typically exercise the option – but rather trades the option for its intrinsic value.

CHAPTER 8

Covered Calls

Puts and calls are like the DNA of financial engineering. There are numerous ways to combine puts and calls into trading strategies, however, the only strategy we will cover in this book is probably the simplest and most conservative option strategy – the covered call. When coupled with a rolling stock strategy, the covered call is a sexy and yet conservative option strategy. A "covered call" is an income-producing strategy where you sell, or "write", call options against shares of stock you already own. We will give some real life examples of how to make money with covered calls. It is so easy, you are going to second guess yourself thinking it's illegal, but trust me – it is perfectly legal.

Anyone can be a covered writer, even yours truly. If you own a stock and you are somewhat neutral on the stock over the short term, then a covered call may be a great option. Typically, you'll sell one contract for every 100 shares of stock. In exchange for selling the call options, you collect an option premium. However, the premium comes with an obligation. If the call option you sold is exercised by the buyer, you may be obligated to deliver your shares of the underlying stock.

Fortunately, since you already own the underlying stock, your potential obligation is "covered" – hence this strategy's name, "covered call" writing. Like all strategies, covered calls are subject to transaction costs. This strategy involves two trades and, therefore, has two commissions: one to purchase the stock and one to sell the call.

"As a man sow, shall he reap/and I know that talk is cheap/But the heat of the battle is as sweet as the victory" - *Bob Marley*

49

If the stock price remains stable or increases, then the writer will be able to keep this income as a profit, even though the profit may have been higher if no call were written. The risk of stock ownership is not eliminated. If the stock price declines, then the net position will likely lose money.

Buying Options

Before I send you off to trade options, you should probably understand a little more about trading options. Execution is extremely important to the covered call writer. The biggest challenge for me is trying to buy an illiquid option. The bid/ask spread of these options is so large that is sometimes difficult to understand where the actual price should be. You may try the Black-Scholes formula to see where the theoretical price of the option should be – that is theoretical, but it gives you the basis for a starting point.

Limit orders are a must when placing these trades. Even though you are guaranteed immediate execution with market orders, you have no control over where the order will be filled. When the option is illiquid and the spread is wide - I usually stay far away. However, if I really feel adventurous, I will put in an offer at the bid or just above the bid. The table below shows an example of the Whole Foods Market (WFM) option chain for the March 2017 options.

WFM Expiration Month - March 2017

Calls						Strike	Puts					
Last	Chg	Bid	Ask	Vol	OpInt		Last	Chg	Bid	Ask	Vol	OpInt
2.1	0	1.99	2.2	0	1,852	30.00	0.07	0	0.05	0.1	0	2,684
1.65	0	1.55	1.74	0	64	30.50	0.15	0	0.09	0.15	0	372
1.16	0	1.16	1.3	0	3,980	31.00	0.22	0	0.19	0.23	0	468
0.93	0	0.82	0.95	0	555	31.50	0.36	0	0.34	0.38	0	116
0.63	0	0.59	0.68	0	1,810	32.00	0.57	0	0.57	0.62	0	347
0.4	0	0.41	0.49	0	620	32.50	0.94	0	0.86	0.95	0	15
0.3	0	0.28	0.33	0	2,327	33.00	1.47	0	1.2	1.34	0	44

"The greatness of a man is not in how much wealth he acquires, but in his integrity and his ability to affect those around him positively." - Bob Marley

0.22	0	0.2	0.27	0	42	33.50	0	0	1.58	1.8	0	0
0.15	0	0.15	0.2	0	3,447	34.00	3.37	0	2.01	2.3	0	16
0	0	0	0.23	0	0	34.50	0	0	2.48	2.77	0	0
0.05	0	0.05	0.1	0	520	35.00	3.47	0	2.8	3.45	0	1
0.06	0	0	0.2	0	16	35.50	0	0	3.3	3.85	0	0
0.04	0	0	0.18	0	101	36.00	0	0	3.75	5.15	0	0
0	0	0	0.19	0	0	36.50	0	0	4.3	6.8	0	0

Let's talk about how you would read the columns in the table above.

Column 1 – Last: This is the last recorded price at which the option was traded.

Column 2 – Chg: This is today's change in the price of the option since the market opened.

Column 3 - The "bid" price is the latest price offered by a market maker to buy a particular option. This means that if you enter a "market order" to sell the March 2017, $30 call, you would sell it at the bid price of $1.99.

Column 4 - Ask: The "ask" price is the latest price offered by a market maker to sell a particular option. This means is that if you enter a "market order" to buy the March 2017, $125 call, you would buy it at the ask price of $2.20.

Column 5 – Volume: This simply tells you how many contracts of a particular option were traded during the latest session. Typically – though not always - options with large volume will have relatively tighter bid/ask spreads as the competition to buy and sell these options is great.

Column 6 – Open Interest: This value indicates the total number of contracts of a particular option that have been opened but have not yet been offset.

Column 7 – Strike: The "strike price" for the option in question. This is the price at which the buyer of that option can purchase the underlying security if he chooses to exercise his option. It is also the price at which the writer of the option must sell the underlying security, if the option is exercised against him.

It is easy to get confused between open interest and trading volume. Trading volume is the number of option contracts being exchanged between buyers and sellers, and it measures the activity of options contracts. For example, in the first row of the table above, the trading volume in call option WFM with a strike price of $30 and an expiration date in March 2017 did not trade any contracts for the day when we pulled the data. Therefore, the trading volume is 0.

Open interest is the number of option contracts that are still open and held by traders and investors. These options have not been closed out, expired or exercised. For example, the open interest in WFM is 1852 at the $30 strike price. This means that investors bought 1852 call options contracts, and some other investors sold 1852 option contracts. The open interest of this particular call option is 1852.

Why write covered calls?

The covered call is an income generating strategy. If you are planning to own the stock for a couple months, why not rent it out? It's like owning an apartment in NY City but not being in it for two to three months – you can easily place it on Airbnb and collect some rental income, otherwise the apartment is just sitting idle. By selling (writing) covered calls, you're usually hoping to keep your shares of the underlying stock while generating extra income via the option premium. Of course, you want the stock price to remain below your strike price, so that the option buyer will not be motivated to exercise the option and grab your shares away from you. If the stock price remains below your strike price, the options will expire worthless, you'll keep the entire option premium at expiration and you'll also keep your shares of the underlying stock. That is a big win for you.

If your stock's price is trading sideways or going down slightly, you will still earn extra income on your long position. However, you now own the stock, so my guess is that you will want the stock price to increase – just not enough to hit your covered call's strike price. But, what the heck – even if you get assigned – you still end up a winner.

What is "assignment"?

If you sell a covered call, you are accepting an obligation to deliver the underlying shares of stock to the buyer at a certain price in exchange for the option premium you collected. If the price of the stock goes up in the favor of the option buyer, the buyer may choose to exercise the option. In this case, we say the shares are "called" away from you. In other words, the buyer will give you a call and ask you to honor your obligation. This is an assignment.

"Assignment" happens via a random lottery system run by the Options Clearing Corporation (OCC). When the OCC receives an exercise notice, it's assigned randomly to a member clearing firm. In turn, your brokerage firm randomly assigns exercise notices to short options positions on their books. So it's possible you'll be assigned through this process.

What are the risks in covered call writing?

Although covered call writing is generally considered a fairly conservative option strategy, there are risks. Remember, as a covered call writer you're wearing two hats: You're a call seller, and you're also a stockholder.

Downside risk as a stockholder. If the value of your underlying shares falls significantly, the loss from holding the stock will likely outweigh the gain from the option premium received.

Limited upside as a stockholder. Before selling a covered call, as a stockholder you have unlimited potential upside from owning the stock. When you start writing covered calls, your potential gain from owning the stock is limited to the gain you may realize if the share price reaches the strike price of the option. At some point after this occurs, the shares will likely be "called away" (assigned) and you will sell the shares for the strike price.

Tips for Covered Calls Writing

Tip 1: Keep volatility (likelihood of stock price movement) in mind.

Writing covered calls works best on stocks with options that are exhibiting medium implied volatility. When implied volatility is too low, the option premium you collect will also likely be low. If implied volatility is high, the premiums will also be higher, but there is a trade-off.

Note: implied volatility can only be determined using an options pricing model (Black –Scholes)

Tip 2: Don't panic if you're assigned

If you're called upon to deliver stock, it can come as a surprise. You have to remember that the stock does not know you own it. In the case of rolling stocks, if the stock gets assigned, there is a likelihood that the stock is at the resistance level and you will have the opportunity to buy it again in a few weeks or months. However, if you have developed a sentimental relationship with your stock, you have more choices in this situation than you may realize. Depending on the number of contracts you wrote against your position, you may deliver the most recent and most expensive shares in your portfolio. As a final option – if you prefer not to part with your shares, you may buy them on the open market on margin and deliver them.

Tip 3: Know in advance what you'll do if the stock goes down

As with many rolling stocks purchases, when we buy the stock, we expect it to exhibit some of the same performance we witnessed with many rolling stocks. However, this is not always the case and even though we are bullish – the stock may, at times, fall lower. If and when this happens, it helps to have a plan in place. In these instances, you have more choices than you think. Selling a call doesn't lock you into your position until expiration. You can always buy back the call and remove your obligation to deliver stock. If the stock has dropped since you sold (wrote) the call, you may be able to buy the call back at a lower cost than the initial sale price, making a profit on the option position. The buy-back also removes your obligation to deliver stock if assigned. If you choose, you can then dump your long stock position, thereby preventing further losses if the stock continues to drop.

Tip 4: Before Writing – Do a What-if Analysis ("static" versus "if-called" returns)

As we have stated before, covered calls are a way to earn income on your long stock positions above and beyond any dividends the stock may pay. "Static" and "if-called" returns help you figure out if selling the call makes sense for your investment strategy.

"Static return" on a covered call is the scenario in which the stock price does not budge – it trades sideways – allowing you, as the writer, to keep the premium as income. On the other hand, "if-called return" assumes assignment occurs and you must deliver the stock at the strike price.

You should do the math for both of these scenarios before diving into covered call writing.

"Never invest in a business you can't understand." – *Warren Buffett*

CHAPTER 9

Rolling Stocks and Covered Calls

Many of us are familiar with the Warren Buffett quote that "Derivatives are financial weapons of mass destruction". That quote may be true (after all, who would disagree with the great Warren Buffett), however, in the case of covered calls, you are the writer of the call option. If derivatives are like nuclear weapons – then you are Harry S. Truman.

When you write a covered call, you are actually trading away some or all of the benefits of the upside of the stock in exchange for the certainty of the cash return in the form of the premium. We all know that there are only two things that are guaranteed in life – hint, making a profit is not one of them. This means that when you buy a stock, there are three scenarios that can happen. The stock can go up, it can go down, or it may just trend sideways. So it appears that with covered call writing, you stand a chance of making money two out of three possible ways. We will examine these three scenarios in three illustrations below.

Let's just say, for the purpose of a good argument, that we have convinced you that the rolling stocks strategy is a potentially profitable and solid money making strategy. Let's imagine that rolling stocks are sprinkled throughout your portfolio, and you somehow noticed that there is one rolling stock that is a prime target for a covered call. You fell in love with this trading opportunity because the option premiums are relatively high, and the stock has been rolling between a support price point of $19 and a resistance of $25. The stock is currently trading at $19.50 – so it is a prime target for a trade. Moreover, you like the stock (because you have done your research and due diligence). Now, the only question that remains is which expiration month you should pick. Smartly, you pick the option expiration month that is three months out from todays' date (giving yourself that extra buffer of time), and you also picked the $25 strike price. Your decisions are based on the frequency of the roll and the expected performance of the stock over the next two months. Of course, we expect the stock to continue its roll and go to $25 in the next two months.

What Happens if the Stock Goes Up (by Less that the Strike Price)

Let's go back to our napkin and illustrate our little scenario in a quick table.

Characteristic	Observation
Current Stock Price	$19.50
Frequency of Roll	Every 2 months
Support Price	$19
Resistance Price	$25
Option Strike Price	$25
Option Premium	$2.50
Time to Expiration	3 months

You bought 100 shares of the stock at $19.50 per share and sold the call option, collecting the $2.50 premium. Over the next two months, the stock performed exactly as you thought it would and continued its boring rolling, advancing to a price of $24.50. So, let's go back to our napkin and review our profit scenario.

Scenario	Money Out	Money In
Bought 100 shares @$19.50	$1,950	
Sold Call Option @$2.50 (Premium)		$250
Sold stock @ $24.50 (3 months later)		$2,450
Total	$1,950	$2,700

"It takes 20 years to build a reputation and five minutes to ruin it. If you think about that, you'll do things differently." – *Warren Buffett*

Net Gain	$700	

The above scenario seems rosy and profitable, but the trade could have gone the other way and not completely in our favor. You know the old cliché – only taxes and death are guaranteed. Losses cannot be prevented but merely reduced in a covered call position. Let's review an alternate scenario where the stock falls after you bought it.

What happens if the stock shoots to the moon and you get assigned

Let's review the scenario where the stock shoots up much more than you expected and you get assigned. In this case, the price of the stocks goes much higher than the strike price of the option. If I was the owner of the option (the option buyer), I would exercise my call option because buying the stock for the strike price is cheaper than buying the stock in the open market. This is called being "in-the-money". In this scenario, your shares will mostly likely be called away from you. You might be sad to part with your stock and miss out on some of those gains - but the scenario holds some benefits for you. Let's setup an illustration to review this scenario where the stock price at the time of expiration is $30.00.

Scenario	Money Out	Money In
Bought 100 shares @$19.50	$1,950	
Sold Call Option @$2.50 (Premium)		$250
Stock Assigned @ $25.00 Strike Price (3 months later)		$2500
Total	$1,950	$2,750
Net Gain	$750	

Even though the stock went to $30.00, your profit was capped at $25.00 (the option strike price). Your net gain is limited. However, as the covered call writer, you haven't made out too badly. When you sold the call, the stock was $19.50, and now you're cashing in at $25.00. That's a profit of 28% on the stock alone. Plus, you get to keep the $2.50 premium you collected when selling the covered call in the first place - an additional 12.8%. Not too shabby. Anytime you enter a covered call position, you must be willing to part with the stock at the strike price. Pick a strike price that will account for enough gains that you won't feel sorry for yourself if your stock gets called away.

What Happens if the Stock Falls Slightly

You bought 100 shares of the stock at $19.50 per share and sold the call option, collecting the $2.50 premium. Over the next two months, the stock trade soured and the stock fell to $17.00. Let's pull out another napkin and review our profit/loss scenario.

Scenario	Money Out	Money In
Bought 100 shares @$19.50	$1,950	
Sold Call Option @$2.50 (Premium)		$250
Current stock price @ $17.94 (3 months later)		$1794
Total	$1,950	$2,044
Net Gain	**$94**	

Even though the stock fell by $1.56 (an 8% drop), your net gain still was $94. You were covered because of the premium you collected up front. However, if the stock had fallen in price by more than $2.00 – you would have been in the red.

What happens if the stock drops like a brick?

We are going to expand our discussion while still using the previous example, but in this case, the stock dropped after you bought it. Let's review the example again – where the stock dropped from $19.50 to $12.50.

"Only buy something that you'd be perfectly happy to hold if the market shut down for 10 years." – *Warren Buffett*

Scenario	Money Out	Money In
Bought 100 shares @$19.50	$1,950	
Sold Call Option @$2.50 (Premium)		$250
Current stock price @ $12.50 (3 months later)		$1250
Total	$1,950	$1500
Net Gain (Loss)	**($450)**	

Unfortunately, your stock fell to $12.50 after you bought it (this would happen only if you were not paying sufficient attention to the earlier chapters and you did not set an appropriate stop loss). If the stock falls by 8% or more, you have the option of buying back the option and making a profit.

What happens if the stock trades sideways?

This is exactly what typically happens with a rolling stock – hence the reason that we like the strategy. A rolling stock may roll sideways between two relatively stable price points for a year or even longer. Sometimes the difference between support and resistance is as small $1.00 or a 10% to 15% price difference. Let's pull out the napkin again and scribble a bit.

Scenario	Money Out	Money In
Bought 100 shares @$19.50	$1,950	
Sold Call Option @$2.50 (Premium)		$250
Current stock price @ $19.75 (3 months later)		$1,975
Total	$1,950	$2,225
Net Gain (Loss)	**$275**	

In the scenario above, your net gain is only $275 – which would represent a 14.1% gain. This gain is coming mainly from the premium you collected from selling the call option.

CHAPTER 10

Rolling Stocks - Case Studies

Just like the surfer who waits patiently for the perfect wave, so does the rolling stocks trader who must wait patiently for the stock to hit the right support price point. The surfer may intuitively calculate several inputs to execute a successful ride to the shore. These include the size of the wave, timing, buoyancy, gravity, friction and hydrodynamic forces. When a wave appears, the surfer will use all their skill and experience to match the speed of the wave and will catch the wave for a glorious ride to shore. Similarly, the rolling stocks trader must analyze market forces, price levels to determine when to jump into a rolling stock.

We have mentioned before that we have looked at thousands of rolling stocks over a twelve year period. Of those thousands of rolling stocks, these cases represent the crème de la crème of the crop of rolling stocks we reviewed and researched. As you review them, we know that you will get super excited as we did when we first stumbled upon this trading strategy. Here's a word of caution. We use a number of different trading strategies, as should you. This rolling stocks strategy, as defined in this book, is only one such strategy. If you are disciplined and you follow the process, your likelihood of making an obscene amount of money will increase dramatically.

Whether you are an aggressive investor or a conservative investor, the rolling stocks strategy presents an exciting opportunity for you to make money. By exercising patience and always knowing your stock positions and price levels, you will keep your rolling stocks methodology well-tuned.

You should always be ready to exploit trading opportunities. The fundamental rules of the rolling stocks trade are the following:

Before You Trade, Determine Your Exit Strategy – You must follow the rules of your road map. We have mentioned that rule earlier in this book; however, it is worth mentioning again. It is important to understand, for each and every trade, what the exit means in terms of dollars and percentage gains before you enter the trade.

We have covered stop losses in some detail – so we probably do not need to mention them here again. However, if you have forgotten, please review that section again.

The Cost of Stocks Matter – If you try to buy the more expensive, your dollars will not stretch very far. It is more prudent to focus on lower priced stocks than on more expensive stocks. As you will come to learn by reviewing the charts in the case studies, lower price stocks will typically roll more frequently and may, in fact, give you a higher percentage return.

Be Smart – Do you recall the Warren Buffett quote "Only buy something that you'd be perfectly happy to hold if the market shut down for 10 years." Trade smart and do not be greedy. In theory, you can look at a historical chart and claim that you could have bought at the bottom and sold at the top. We all know that this is fool's gold. Don't be fooled that you will always get into a trade at the bottom and then sell at the top. Based on our research, if you capitalize on 50% to 60% of the opportunities – you will still end up a winner.

"It's better to hang out with people better than you. Pick out associates whose behavior is better than yours and you'll drift in that direction." – *Warren Buffett*

AGYS - Agilisys Inc   **MyRollingStocks.com Charts**

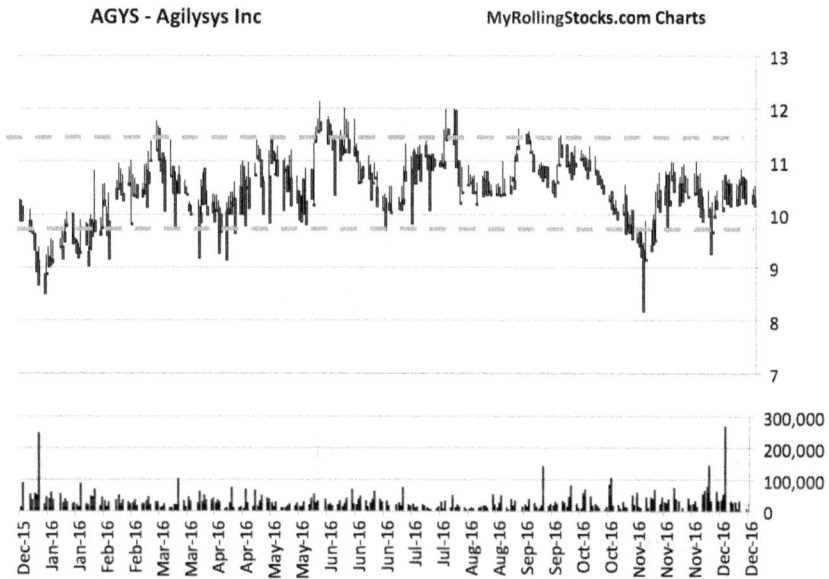

Agilisys, Inc. is a technology company. The company provides software for point-of-sale (POS), property management, inventory and procurement, workforce management, analytics, document management, and mobile and wireless solutions and services to the hospitality industry. The company serves four market sectors: gaming, both corporate and tribal; hotels, resorts and cruise; foodservice management, and restaurants, universities, stadia and healthcare.

AGYS is first on our list because it is one of our all-time favorites. As evidenced by the graph, as rolling stocks go, this one is as gorgeous as the sunset at Rick's Café in Negril, Jamaica. Looking at the graph, it is hard not to be blinded by the luminous glow of the profit potential. The stock has been rolling between $9.90 and $11.30 for over a year. Each roll shows an opportunity of $1.40 – going from $9.90 to $11.30. If we did our quick back of the napkin calculation, a $1.40 gain on a cost basis of $9.90 results in a 14.1% gain. If this was an annual return, the 14.1% gain is impressive. However, a closer examination of the chart shows that there were four opportunities to roll with AGYS. We could have completed a $1.40 gain four (4) times in a twelve-month period. Let's flip the napkin and continue with that math calculation. The four rolls would have resulted in a $5.60 gain and with a cost basis of $9.90 – this is a 56.6% gain in a twelve-month period.

AGYS Share Related Items	
Market Cap (Mil) $	252.71
Shares Outstanding (Mil)	23.4
Float (Mil)	22.29
Beta	0.79
Per Share Data	
Earnings TTM	-0.35
Sales TTM	5.63
Book Value MRQ	5.16
Cash Flow TTM	-0.17

Mil = Million * MRQ = Most Recent Quarter * TTM = Trailing Twelve Month

TACT - Transact Technologies Inc   MyRollingstocks.com Charts

TransAct Technologies Incorporated (TransAct) designs, develops and sells market-specific solutions, including printers, terminals, software and other products for transaction-based and other industries. The company operates through the segment, which includes design, development, assembly and marketing of transaction printers and terminals, and providing printer and terminal related software, services, supplies and spare parts.

In a twelve-month period, TACT showed us three clear buying opportunities. There were also two opportunities to roll TACT over that period. TACT was rolling between support of $6.75 and a resistance of $8. That profit spread represents an 18.5% gain.

TACT Share Related Items	
Market Cap (Mil) $	49.47
Shares Outstanding (Mil)	7.38
Float (Mil)	6.87
Beta	0.74
Per Share Data	
Earnings TTM	0.36
Sales TTM	7.18
Book Value MRQ	3.19
Cash Flow TTM	0.53

Mil = Million * MRQ = Most Recent Quarter * TTM = Trailing Twelve Month

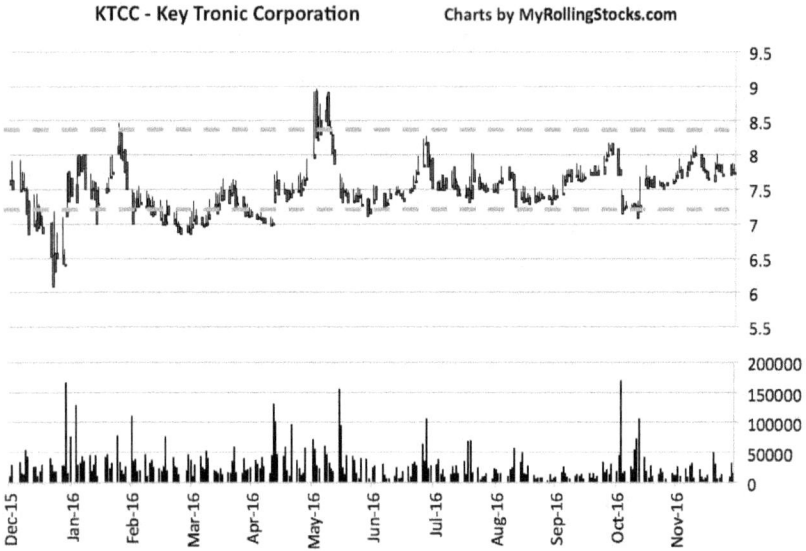

KTCC - Key Tronic Corporation   Charts by MyRollingStocks.com

Key Tronic Corporation, doing business as KeyTronicEMS Co., is engaged in contract manufacturing for a range of products. The company provides electronic manufacturing services (EMS) and solutions to original equipment manufacturers (OEMs) of a range of products. The company provides engineering services, procurement and distribution, materials management, manufacturing and assembly services, in-house testing, and customer service.

KTCC was rolling in a tight trading range. The stock was rolling between $7.25 and $8.25. Over the twelve-month period, there were at least twelve opportunities to buy the stock at the support. There were opportunities to roll the stock five times in that time period – each time with an approximate potential profit of $1.00. Let's go back to our napkin and calculate the potential profit. In this case, we will be conservative and assume that we only could get 75% of the gains. That means, we could profit $3.75 over the five trades for a 52% gain. Even a clean hedge fund magnate would admit that that is still impressive.

KTCC Share Related Items	
Market Cap (Mil) $	84.08
Shares Outstanding (Mil)	10.76
Float (Mil)	10.05
Beta	0.5
Per Share Data	
Earnings TTM	0.67
Sales TTM	42.66
Book Value MRQ	9.9
Cash Flow TTM	1.23

Mil = Million * MRQ = Most Recent Quarter * TTM = Trailing Twelve Month

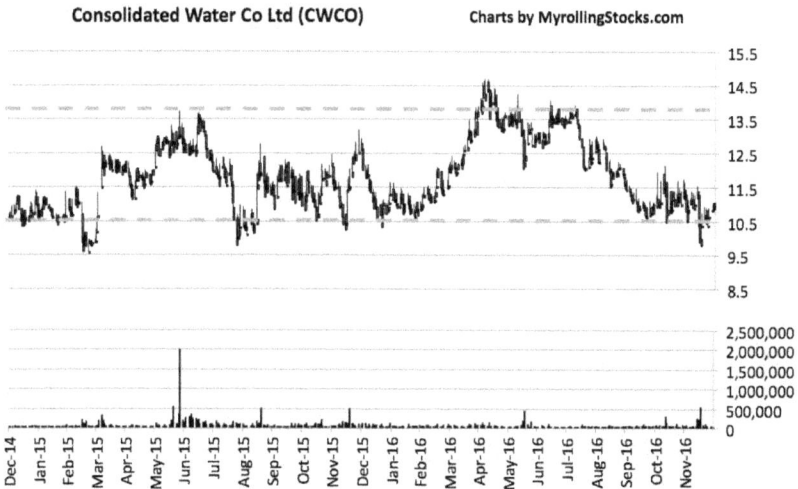

Consolidated Water Co Ltd (CWCO)   Charts by MyrollingStocks.com

Consolidated Water Co. Ltd. (CWCO) develops and operates seawater desalination plants that utilize reverse osmosis technology and water distribution systems in areas where naturally occurring supplies of potable water are scarce or non-existent. The company operates in three segments:

"Price is what you pay. Value is what you get." – *Warren Buffett* retail water operations, bulk water operations and services operations. The retail water operations segment produces and supplies water to end users, including residential, commercial and government customers. The bulk water operations segment produces potable water from seawater and sells this water to governments and private customers.

CWCO is the only stock on this list that has a time frame of 24 months. CWCO has been rolling between $10.50 and $13.50 for almost 24 months. If you bought in at $10.50 and the stock went to $13.50 – that would be a 28.6% gain. At this point, there is hardly much more to say – we should drop the mic and walk off the stage. However, in reviewing the charts, there were two additional opportunities to execute the same trade on CWCO.

CWCO Share Related Items	
Market Cap (Mil) $	160.78
Shares Outstanding (Mil)	14.82
Float (Mil)	14.51
Beta	0.8
Per Share Data	
Earnings TTM	0.27
Sales TTM	3.84
Book Value MRQ	9.76
Cash Flow TTM	N/A

Mil = Million * MRQ = Most Recent Quarter * TTM = Trailing Twelve Months

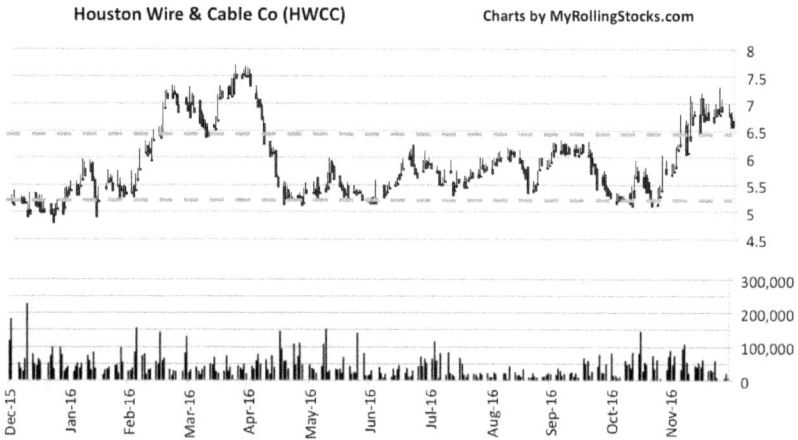

Houston Wire & Cable Co (HWCC) Charts by MyRollingStocks.com

Houston Wire & Cable Company (HWCC) is a holding company. The company is engaged in the provision of electrical and mechanical wire and cable, hardware and related services. It operates through sales of wire and cable, hardware and related services segments in the United States market. Its cable management program includes purchasing and storing inventory for product availability.

HWCC has been a mainstay on our list of prominent rolling stocks. It can be classified as rolling stocks royalty for its consistency in the rolling stocks category. This stock has consistently rolled between $5.25 and $6.50 for the better part of a year. By looking at the graph, you will observe that the stock has faithfully hung to its support line like Barack Obama to Michelle. It is a beautiful sight. Even though there were only three opportunities to roll this stock, it still presented a wonderful trading opportunity.

HWCC Share Related Items	
Market Cap (Mil) $	108.93
Shares Outstanding (Mil)	16.38
Float (Mil)	15.95
Beta	1.37

"Time is the friend of the wonderful company, the enemy of the mediocre."
– Warren Buffett

Per Share Data	
Earnings TTM	-0.27
Sales TTM	15.97
Book Value MRQ	5.61
Cash Flow TTM	-0.09

Mil = Million * MRQ = Most Recent Quarter * TTM = Trailing Twelve Months

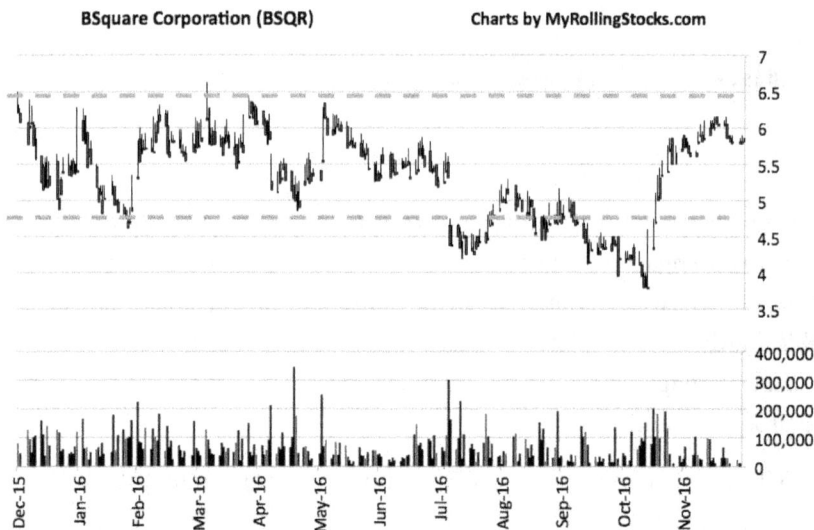

BSquare Corporation (BSQR)   Charts by MyRollingStocks.com

BSQUARE Corporation (BSQR) resells software from Microsoft Corporation (MSFT) and provides software solutions and related engineering services to companies that develop smart, connected systems. A smart, connected system is a dedicated purpose computing device that typically has a display, runs an operating system and is connected to a network or data cloud through a wired or wireless connection.

BSQR rolled between $4.75 and $6.40 for a year. It presented us with four opportunities to roll the stock. Based on the graph shown, the first opportunity to roll the stock was in January of 2016. The first roll would have netted a profit of $1.20. Subsequent rolls would have been equally lucrative.

BSQR Share Related Items	
Market Cap (Mil) $	74.09
Shares Outstanding (Mil)	12.45
Float (Mil)	11.56
Beta	2.11
Per Share Data	
Earnings TTM	0.11
Sales TTM	7.69
Book Value MRQ	3.12
Cash Flow TTM	0.16

Mil = Million * MRQ = Most Recent Quarter * TTM = Trailing Twelve Months

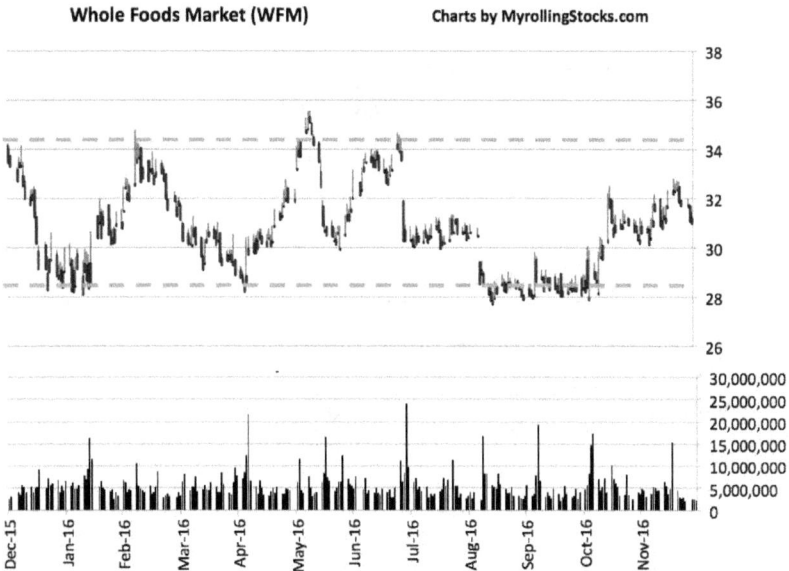

Whole Foods Market (WFM)   Charts by MyrollingStocks.com

Whole Foods Market, Inc. (WFM) is engaged in the business of natural and organic foods supermarkets. The company operates approximately 456 stores in the United States, Canada and the United Kingdom. Its stores have an average size of approximately 39,000 square feet and are supported by its distribution centers, bake house facilities, commissary kitchens, seafood-processing facilities, a produce procurement center, and a specialty coffee and tea procurement and roasting operation.

You may have noticed that we used WFM in an earlier example. It has been one of our favorite rolling stocks. Over the course of one year, WFM presented at least 10 opportunities to buy the stock at the support. Anyone could have bought this stock at $28 in January 2016 and sold it in March 2016 for $34. Typically this stock was rolling every 2 months. There are four clear rolls presented in the graph of WSM; each roll had the potential of netting $6 in profit. In this case, our four rolls could have netted $24. If you net $24 using the same resident $28 in cost each time – that is a net profit of 85.7%.

WFM Share Related Items	
Market Cap (Mil) $	9,835.55
Shares Outstanding (Mil)	318.41
Float (Mil)	315.1
Beta	0.76
Per Share Data	
Earnings TTM	1.55
Sales TTM	48.22
Book Value MRQ	10.13
Cash Flow TTM	3.08

Mil = Million * MRQ = Most Recent Quarter * TTM = Trailing Twelve Months

IXYS Corporation (IXYS)   **Charts by MyRollingStocks.com**

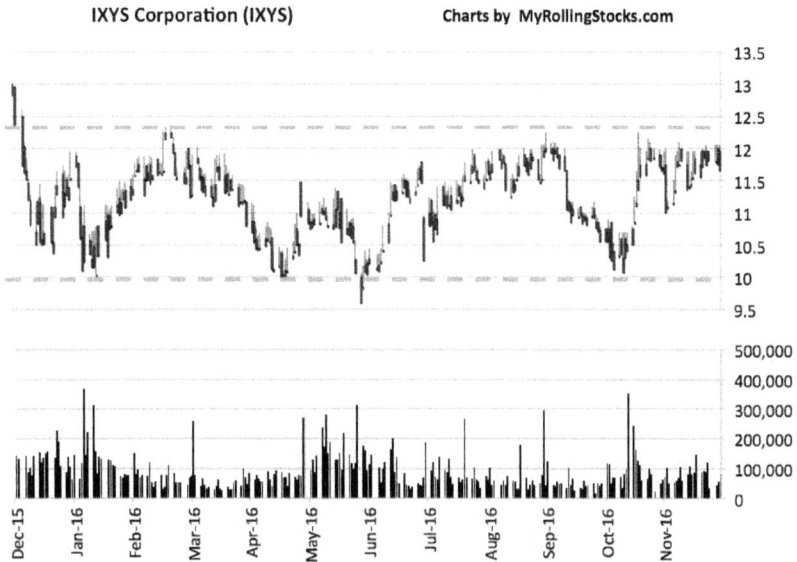

IXYS Corporation (IXYS) is a multi-market integrated semiconductor company. The company is engaged in the development, manufacture and marketing of power semiconductors, mixed-signal integrated circuits (ICs), application specific integrated circuits (ASICs), microcontrollers, systems and radio frequency (RF) power semiconductors. Its power semiconductors are sold separately and are also packaged in high power modules that consist of multiple semiconductor dies.

IXYS is another beautiful image of a rolling stock. This stock showed us at least seven (7) buying opportunities over a twelve-month period. A quick conservative review showed that we could have rolled this stock three times in the twelve months. The stock was rolling between a support of $10.25 and a resistance of $12. Therefore, each roll could have resulted in a $1.75 profit. The back of the napkin showed that a 17.1% profit on each roll of the stock is not far-fetched. If this stock was rolled three times – then our profit potential would have been 51.2%.

"Open your eyes, look within. Are you satisfied with the life you're living?"
- Bob Marley

IXYS Share Related Items	
Market Cap (Mil) $	373.71
Shares Outstanding (Mil)	31.54
Float (Mil)	24.73
Beta	0.96
Per Share Data	
Earnings TTM	0.48
Sales TTM	9.77
Book Value MRQ	9.06
Cash Flow TTM	0.86

Mil = Million * MRQ = Most Recent Quarter * TTM = Trailing Twelve Month

International Speedway Corp (ISCA)   Charts by MyRollingStocks.com

International Speedway Corporation (ISCA) is an owner of motorsports entertainment facilities and a promoter of motorsports themed entertainment activities. Its event operations consist of racing events at its motorsports entertainment facilities. This includes providing catering and food and beverage concessions at its facilities that host National Association for Stock Car Auto Racing (NASCAR) Sprint Cup Series events. It owns and/or operates over 10 motorsports entertainment facilities.

As we reviewed the myriad of rolling stocks that would eventually be filtered to produce this list, we were in a quandary about ISCA. Why? Should ISCA actually make the final cut? The other stocks on the list are like Richard Petty, Dale Earnhardt, and Jeff Gordon – they know how to play in the pocket. This stock is like Elliott Sadler – a good driver who needs to learn a few fundamentals. ISCA has been rolling between a support of $31.50 and a resistance $36 over the period of one year. ISCA showed us three opportunities to roll the stock – each roll would have produced a $4.50 profit. The three rolls, if the entire profit margin opportunity was exploited, would have produced a profit of $13.50. This $13.50 over three rolls translates into 42.86% profit.

ISCA Share Related Items	
Market Cap (Mil) $	1,705.24
Shares Outstanding (Mil)	45.64
Float (Mil)	27.17
Beta	1.25
Per Share Data	
Earnings TTM	1.64
Sales TTM	14.22
Book Value MRQ	30.57
Cash Flow TTM	3.78

Mil = Million * MRQ = Most Recent Quarter * TTM = Trailing Twelve Months

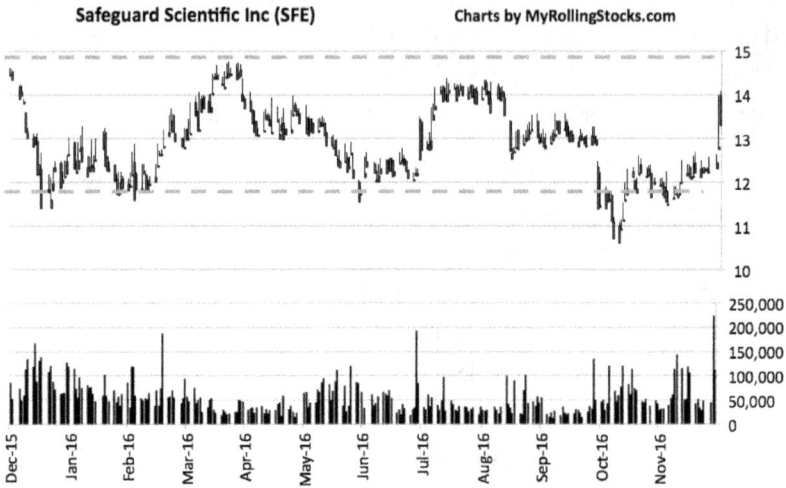

Safeguard Scientifics, Inc. (SFE) provides capital, as well as strategic, operational and management resources to growth-stage businesses. The company participates in early- and growth-stage financings. It operates through two segments: Healthcare and Technology. The Healthcare segment's companies focus principally on medical technology (MedTech), including diagnostics and devices, and healthcare technology (HealthTech). The Technology segment's companies focus principally on digital media, financial technology (FinTech), and enterprise software, including mobile technology, cloud, Internet of Things (IoT) and big data.

As you can obviously see from the graph, SFE is a beautiful rolling stock. If only we could measure beauty on the same scale – we would say "move over Scarlett Johansson". It showed us upwards of 8 buying opportunities and gave us three (3) opportunities to roll the stock between the support of $11.55 and $14.00. Assuming that we would have been able to roll this three times, the profit spread per roll of $2.45 – would have resulted in a $7.35 gain and a total profit of 63.6%

"If you don't pay appropriate attention to what has your attention, it will take more of your attention than it deserves." – *David Allen*

SFE Share Related Items	
Market Cap (Mil) $	269.17
Shares Outstanding (Mil)	20.24
Float (Mil)	19.9
Beta	1.32
Per Share Data	
Earnings TTM	-0.92
Sales TTM	0
Book Value MRQ	9.44
Cash Flow TTM	N/A

Mil = Million * MRQ = Most Recent Quarter * TTM = Trailing Twelve Months

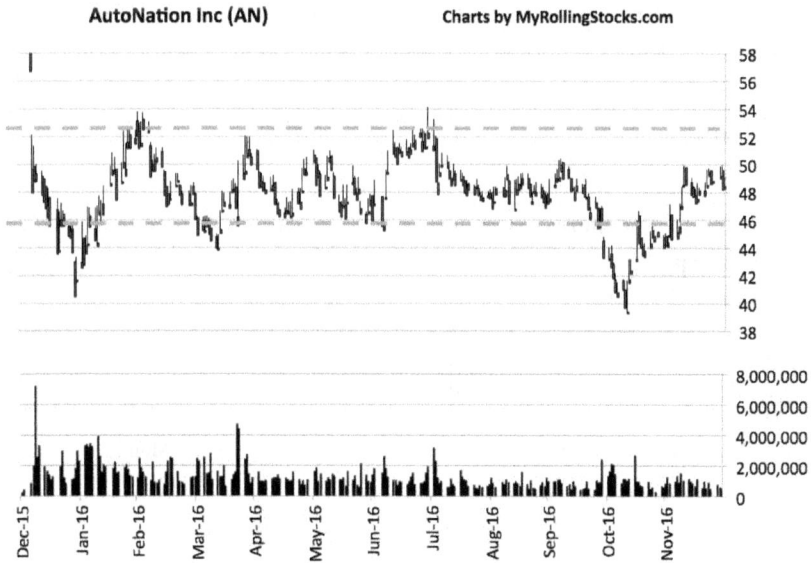

AutoNation Inc (AN)   Charts by MyRollingStocks.com

AutoNation, Inc. (AN) is an automotive retailer in the United States. The company offers a range of automotive products and services, including new vehicles, used vehicles, parts and service, which includes automotive repair

"Take time to deliberate; but when the time for action arrives, stop thinking and go in." - *Napoleon Bonaparte*

and maintenance services, as well as wholesale parts and collision businesses, and automotive finance and insurance products, including vehicle service and other protection products, as well as the arranging of financing for vehicle purchases through third-party finance sources. It operates through three segments, including Domestic, Import and Premium Luxury.

The graph of AN shows a similarly gorgeous rolling stock. Over a twelve-month period, AN showed us four opportunities to roll the stock with the first roll and buying opportunity occurring in January of 2016. The stock was rolling between a support of $45.00 and a resistance price point of $52.50. The spread of $7.50 between support and resistance could have been realized four times in that twelve month period. If realized, the total annual profit gain would have been a 67% gain.

Share Related Items	
Market Cap (Mil) $	4,979.45
Shares Outstanding (Mil)	101.04
Float (Mil)	88.84
Beta	1.05
Per Share Data	
Earnings TTM	3.9
Sales TTM	201.86
Book Value MRQ	21.94
Cash Flow TTM	5.21

Mil = Million * MRQ = Most Recent Quarter * TTM = Trailing Twelve Months

Gigamedia Ltd (GIGM)   Charts by MyRollingStocks.com

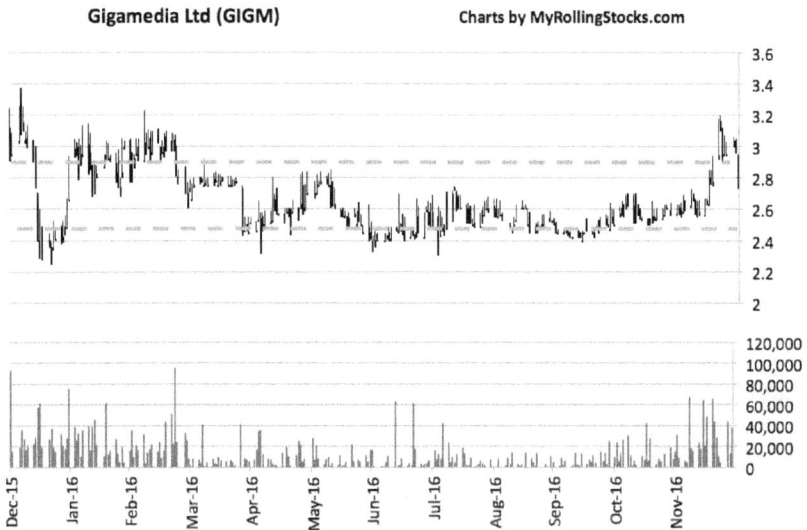

GigaMedia Limited (GIGM) is a holding company with a portfolio of businesses providing online games and cloud computing services. The company operates through two segments: Asian online game and service, and cloud service business. The company has online game operations in Taiwan, Hong Kong and Macau and a cloud computing software and service business based in Taipei. In online games, the company owns and operates FunTown, an online game portal in Taiwan and Hong Kong. In cloud computing, it owns and operates GigaCloud, a provider of cloud computing solutions and related services focused on the cloud services market for small- and medium-sized enterprises (SMEs) in Taiwan.

GIGM has been rolling between a support price point of $2.40 and a resistance of $2.85. In the twelve-month time frame, the stock offered three opportunities to roll. The first opportunity occurred in January 2016 when the stock bounced from $2.10 to $3.20 in less than one month. The subsequent rolls were less exciting and more constrained. However, an investor who bought in on the second roll in May 2016 at $2.40 would have seen the stock rise to $2.85 – a $0.45 gain which is an 18.7% gain. Not shabby!

"Do the hard jobs first. The easy jobs will take care of themselves."
– *Dale Carnegie*

GIGM Share Related Items	
Market Cap (Mil) $	31.61
Shares Outstanding (Mil)	11.05
Float (Mil)	7.12
Beta	1.41
Per Share Data	
Earnings TTM	-1.42
Sales TTM	0.92
Book Value MRQ	5.7
Cash Flow TTM	-1.13

Mil = Million * MRQ = Most Recent Quarter * TTM = Trailing Twelve Month

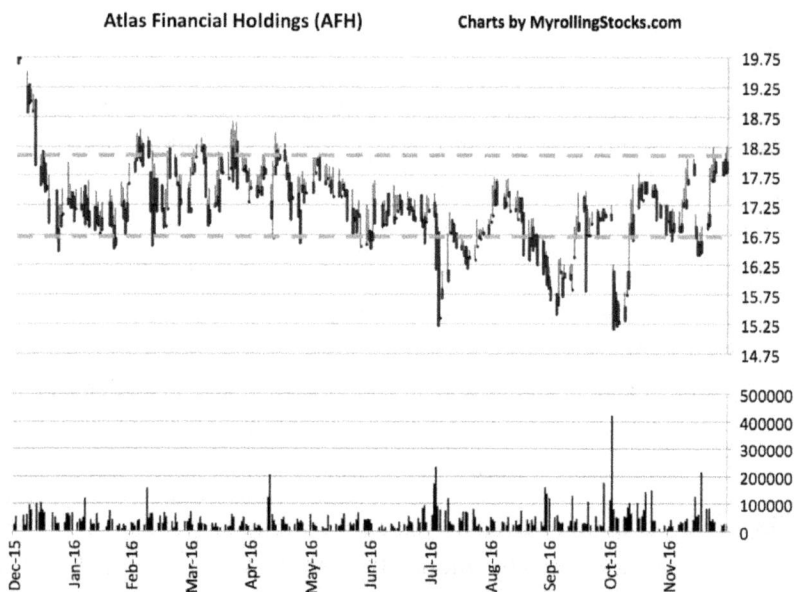

Atlas Financial Holdings (AFH)   Charts by MyrollingStocks.com

Atlas Financial Holdings, Inc. is a financial services holding company. The company, through its subsidiaries, is engaged in the underwriting of commercial automobile insurance policies, focusing on the light commercial automobile sector, which includes taxi cabs, non-emergency para-transit, limousine, livery and business auto. The company operates through the property and casualty (P&C) insurance business segment. It develops and delivers specialty insurance products, which are distributed to the insured through a network of independent retail agents utilizing its operating platform.

AFH presented multiple buying opportunities in the twelve month period starting in December 2015. We counted at least 14 opportunities (at a minimum) in that period. The stock has been rolling for a year between $16.50 and $18.00. In January 2016, an investor could have bought the stock at $16.50 and sold it a month later for $18.25, which is a 10.6% gain. The investor could have done that six times in the twelve-month period. If that was done, that stick-to-itiveness would have gained a whopping 63.6% before all the transaction costs.

AFH Share Related Items	
Market Cap (Mil) $	214.01
Shares Outstanding (Mil)	12.02
Float (Mil)	10.84
Beta	1.07
Per Share Data	
Earnings TTM	1.59
Sales TTM	13.7
Book Value MRQ	12.19
Cash Flow TTM	1.71

Mil = Million * MRQ = Most Recent Quarter * TTM = Trailing Twelve Months

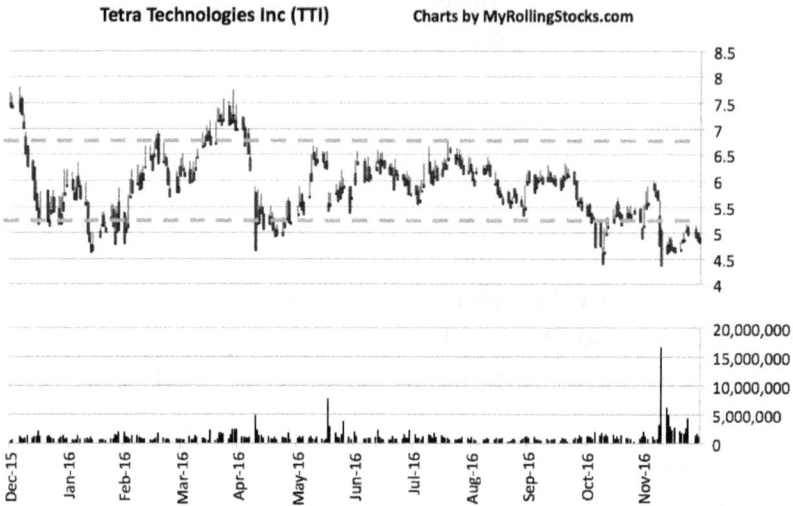

Tetra Technologies Inc (TTI)   Charts by MyRollingStocks.com

TETRA Technologies, Inc. (TTI) is an oil and gas services company. The company focuses on completion fluids and associated products and services, water management, production well testing, offshore rig cooling, compression services and equipment, and offshore services, such as decommissioning and diving. It is composed of five segments organized into four divisions: Fluids, Production Testing, Compression and Offshore. The Fluids division manufactures and markets clear brine fluids, additives and associated products and services to the oil and gas industry.

TTI is another one of our favorites. Without going into much detail, we hope you can see why. The stock presented at least five (5) buying opportunities and at least two full rolls. In those two rolling opportunities, you could have bought this stock at $5.00 and sold it for $6.50 – a gain of $1.50 each time. If you were able to gain $3.00 on this stock over the 12-month time period and use the cost basis of $5.00 – that represents a 60% gain. By this point, after reviewing these graphs, the potency of this trading strategy is beginning to have the same intoxicating effect it had on us.

TTI Share Related Items	
Market Cap (Mil) $	578.48
Shares Outstanding (Mil)	112.76
Float (Mil)	109.9
Beta	1.05
Per Share Data	
Earnings TTM	-3.44
Sales TTM	9.38
Book Value MRQ	1.96
Cash Flow TTM	-3.55

Mil = Million * MRQ = Most Recent Quarter * TTM = Trailing Twelve Months

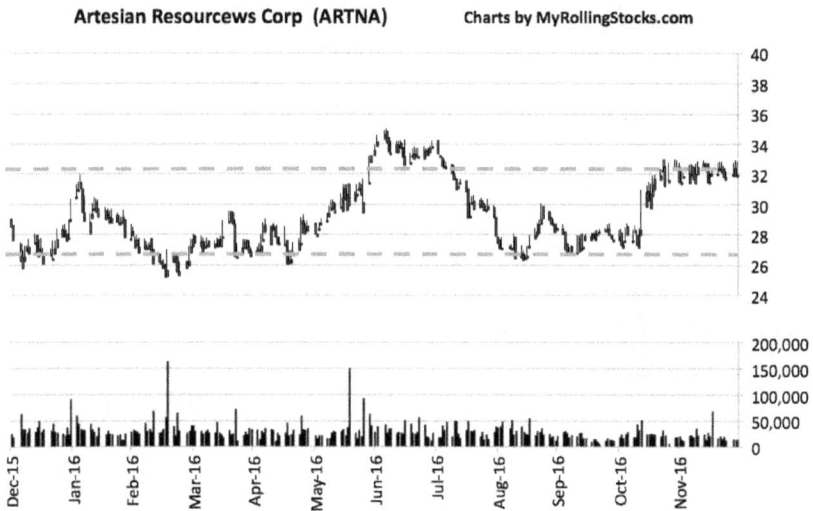

Artesian Resourcews Corp (ARTNA)   Charts by MyRollingStocks.com

Artesian Resources Corporation (ARTNA) is a holding company. The company, through its subsidiaries, offers water, wastewater and other services on the Delmarva Peninsula. It distributes and sells water, including water for public and private fire protection, to residential, commercial, industrial, municipal and utility customers in Delaware, Maryland and

Pennsylvania. It also provides contract water and wastewater operations, and water and sewer Service Line Protection Plans.

ARTNA showed three opportunities to roll from a support of $26 up to the resistance of $32. Those opportunities represent a $6 gain for each roll. Let's just say that you were able to capitalize on the roll in each of those cases, you could be making profits until you were completely bored. The $6 gain represents a 23% gain. If we extrapolate that gain to the entire year – we would have $18 – while all the time still utilizing our $26 cost basis. The quick back-of-the-envelope math suggests that this is a 69% gain. Folks, I will challenge you – I cannot find the person who would not get excited by a 69% gain.

ARTNA Share Related Items	
Market Cap (Mil) $	281.7
Shares Outstanding (Mil)	9.12
Float (Mil)	8.17
Beta	0.18
Per Share Data	
Earnings TTM	1.32
Sales TTM	8.58
Book Value MRQ	14.91
Cash Flow TTM	2.31

Mil = Million * MRQ = Most Recent Quarter * TTM = Trailing Twelve Months

UT Starcom Holdings (UTSI) Charts by MyRollingStocks.com

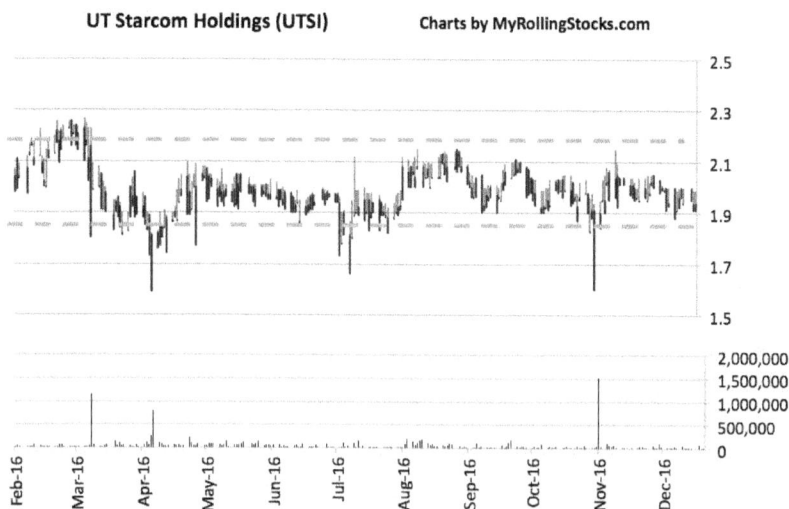

UTStarcom Holdings Corp. (UTSI) provides broadband products, solution and services. The company delivers broadband transport and access (both wireless fidelity (Wi-Fi) and fixed line) products and solutions that are optimized for mobile backhaul, metro aggregation, broadband access and Wi-Fi data offloading. Its segments include Equipment, which is focused on its equipment sales, including network infrastructure and application products, and Services, which is engaged in providing services and support of its equipment products and also the new operational support segment.

UTSI is another stock – which was just waiting for someone to pluck the profits. Let's take a minute to review the chart. UTSI was rolling between $1.80 and $2.10 for the majority of the period. We counted three opportunities to gain at least $0.20 on this stock over the period. The first buying opportunity was in March, 2016. Subsequent opportunities presented themselves throughout the course of the year.

UTSI Share Related Items	
Market Cap (Mil) $	71.1
Shares Outstanding (Mil)	36.46
Float (Mil)	24.34
Beta	-0.06
Per Share Data	
Earnings TTM	-0.3
Sales TTM	2.35
Book Value MRQ	2.58
Cash Flow TTM	-0.26

Mil = Million * MRQ = Most Recent Quarter * TTM = Trailing Twelve Months

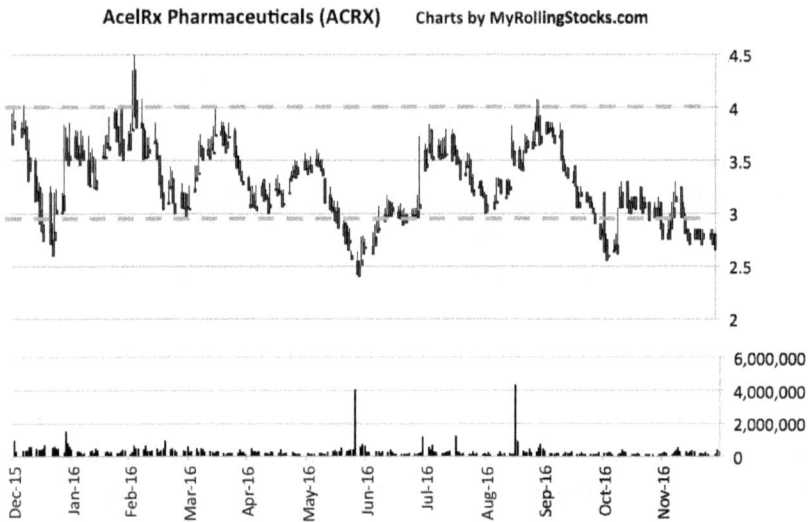

AcelRx Pharmaceuticals (ACRX)   Charts by MyRollingStocks.com

AcelRx Pharmaceuticals, Inc. (ACRX) is a pharmaceutical company focused on the development and commercialization of therapies for the treatment of moderate-to-severe acute pain. The company operates through the segment, which includes development and commercialization of product candidates for the treatment of pain. Its lead product candidates include

ARX-04, Zalviso, which utilize sublingual sufentanil, delivered through a non-invasive route of administration, and ARX-03. ARX-04 is meant for the treatment of moderate-to-severe acute pain and is to be administered by a healthcare professional to a patient in medically supervised settings.

ACRX has displayed the attributes of a classic rolling stock. This stock presented multiple opportunities to buy into the stock. Over the period of 12 months, it has rolled between $3.00 and $3.80. We have counted four (4) total rolls of this stock. That is four (4) opportunities to go from $3.00 to $3.80 in a twelve month time period. By this time, you are able to realize the math we will do to calculate the potential opportunity. Four opportunities to gain $0.80 results in a $3.20 total gain. If you recall, we are using $3.00 as our cost basis. If our math is correct, that is a 107% gain. If that profit potential does not excite you, then...

ACRX Share Related Items	
Market Cap (Mil) $	115.6
Shares Outstanding (Mil)	45.33
Float (Mil)	44.34
Beta	2.62
Per Share Data	
Earnings TTM	-0.98
Sales TTM	0.28
Book Value MRQ	0.07
Cash Flow TTM	-0.93

Mil = Million * MRQ = Most Recent Quarter * TTM = Trailing Twelve Months

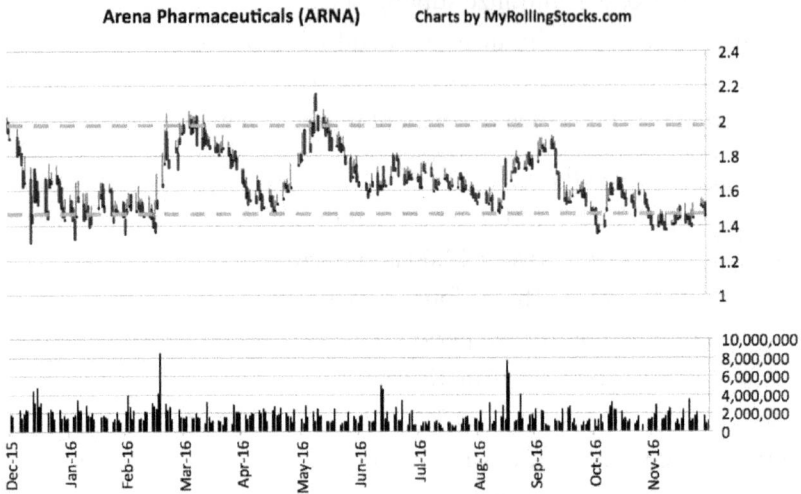

Arena Pharmaceuticals (ARNA)   Charts by MyRollingStocks.com

Arena Pharmaceuticals, Inc. (ARNA) is a biopharmaceutical company focused on discovering, developing and commercializing small molecule drugs that target G protein-coupled receptors (GPCRs). The company's drug, Lorcaserin, is approved for marketing in the United States and South Korea for the indication of weight management, and is being commercialized under the brand name, BELVIQ.

ARNA is another classic rolling stock. The stock consolidated during the first several months of 2016, presenting several buying opportunities while rolling between $1.40 and $1.90. The total opportunity was a $0.50 gain. This graph showed us three (3) opportunities to buy the stock at the support and sell at the resistance. Without accounting for transaction costs – this is total gain of $1.50. Our principal cost basis was $1.40. If (and that is a big "if") we are able to realize the enter bucket of profits ($0.50 in this case) – that represents a 107% gain. Let's just say, for the sake of argument and modesty, that we were only able to gain 60% of that profit potential with each roll opportunity. That is still $0.90 gained on a principal cost basis of $1.40 – that is a 64% gain – which is still not shabby.

ARNA Share Related Items	
Market Cap (Mil) $	357.67
Shares Outstanding (Mil)	243.31
Float (Mil)	242.12
Beta	-0.7
Per Share Data	
Earnings TTM	-0.38
Sales TTM	0.19
Book Value MRQ	0.01
Cash Flow TTM	-0.3

Mil = Million * MRQ = Most Recent Quarter * TTM = Trailing Twelve Months

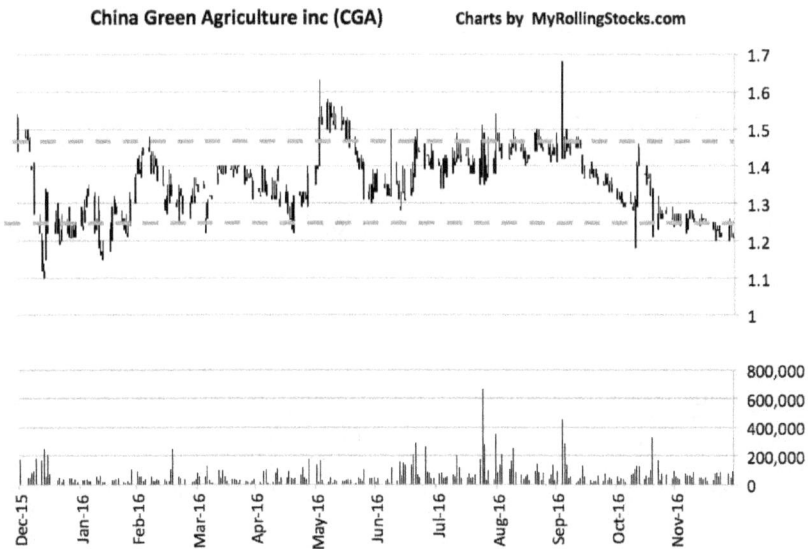

China Green Agriculture inc (CGA)   Charts by MyRollingStocks.com

China Green Agriculture, Inc. (CGA) is engaged in the research, development, production and sale of various types of fertilizers and agricultural products in the People's Republic of China (PRC). It does this through its Chinese subsidiaries Shaanxi TechTeam Jinong Humic Acid Product Co.,

"Concentrate all your thoughts upon the work in hand. The sun's rays do not burn until brought to a focus." - *Alexander Graham Bell*

Ltd. (Jinong) and Beijing Gufeng Chemical Products Co., Ltd. (Gufeng), and its variable interest entity (VIE), Xi'an Hu County Yuxing Agriculture Technology Development Co., Ltd. (Yuxing).

Over the 12 month period shown on the graph, this stock showed us more than twelve (12) opportunities to buy at the support level. That is an average of one opportunity per month. The stock rolled between $1.25 and $1.50 for the better part of 12 months. Based on our other case studies, this stock is displaying an average performance. The profit potential is 20% per roll. Even though there were multiple opportunities to get into the stock, there were three rolls that we can count in the time period selected. That means that if we exploited the entire profit opportunity, we would have made $0.75 using our principal of $1.25. When we last checked, that was a 60% gain.

Share Related Items	
Market Cap (Mil) $	46.31
Shares Outstanding (Mil)	37.65
Float (Mil)	25.49
Beta	0.69
Per Share Data	
Earnings TTM	0.67
Sales TTM	7.45
Book Value MRQ	10.19
Cash Flow TTM	1.66

Mil = Million * MRQ = Most Recent Quarter * TTM = Trailing Twelve Months

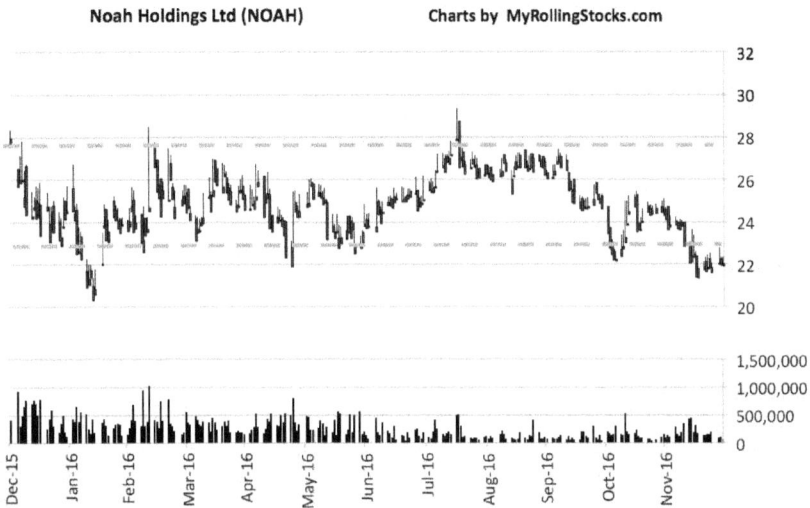

Noah Holdings Ltd (NOAH) Charts by MyRollingStocks.com

Noah Holdings Limited (NOAH) is a wealth management service provider with a focus on global wealth investment and asset allocation services for high net worth individuals and enterprises in China. The company operates through three segments: wealth management, asset management and Internet finance.

This stock presents an exciting opportunity. This is the reason rolling stocks is one of our favorite strategies. It is not our only trading strategy, but it is the favorite. NOAH showed more than 12 opportunities to jump into the stock at the support level. It traded between $22.50 and $27 for the majority of the time period. Let's look at the potential profit opportunities. If you bought this stock at $22.50 and sold it at $27.00 – that would be a 20% gain. You had more than four opportunities to make that profit. Not accounting for the evil transaction cost – that maximum opportunity is an $18 gain using the same principal of $22.50. That is an obscene opportunity to make money – this is similar to trading options but without the messy time-premium and risks.

NOAH Share Related Items	
Market Cap (Mil) $	1,241.33
Shares Outstanding (Mil)	56.25
Float (Mil)	18.59
Beta	2.52
Per Share Data	
Earnings TTM	1.52
Sales TTM	6
Book Value MRQ	8.35
Cash Flow TTM	N/A

Mil = Million * MRQ = Most Recent Quarter * TTM = Trailing Twelve Months

Euroseas Ltd (ESEA)   Charts by MyrollingStocks.com

Euroseas Ltd. (ESEA) is engaged in the shipping business. The company is an owner and operator of dry bulk and container carrier vessels and is a provider of seaborne transportation for dry bulk and containerized cargoes. Eurobulk Ltd. manages the company's operations.

"It is not really work if you are having fun." – *Pierre Omidyar*

ESEA has been rolling in a tight range of $1.65 to $2.80 for the duration of one year. This is a relatively inexpensive stock with relatively stable trading volume. There were multiple opportunities to buy this stock in the $1.65 price range. This stock required that you exercise patience and discipline. Even though this stock had a slower rolling period (if you bought the stock in January 2016, it rose to resistance in May 2016), your potential profit would have been 69.7%. That is not a shabby return for 5 months of "work".

ESEA Share Related Items	
Market Cap (Mil) $	15.81
Shares Outstanding (Mil)	8.28
Float (Mil)	3.51
Beta	2
Per Share Data	
Earnings TTM	-3.98
Sales TTM	3.69
Book Value MRQ	12.29
Cash Flow TTM	-2.87

Mil = Million * MRQ = Most Recent Quarter * TTM = Trailing Twelve Months

Blackberry Inc (BBRY)   Charts by MyRollingStocks.com

BlackBerry Limited (BBRY) provides mobile communications solutions. The company is engaged in the sale of smartphones and enterprise software and services. The company's products and services include enterprise solutions and services, devices, BlackBerry technology solutions and messaging.

A quick review of the graph show that this stock has been rolling for one year with 6 or more buying opportunities at the support level. The stock has been rolling between $6.55 and $8 for the majority of the rolling time period. Based on the annual chart shown above the first buying opportunity was in January 2016. If you were able to capture the complete roll in one trade – you net profit would be 22.13%.

BBRY Share Related Items	
Market Cap (Mil) $	3,679.80
Shares Outstanding (Mil)	529.96
Float (Mil)	529.66
Beta	1.03
Per Share Data	
Earnings TTM	-2.67
Sales TTM	2.84
Book Value MRQ	3.95
Cash Flow TTM	-2.08

Mil = Million * MRQ = Most Recent Quarter * TTM = Trailing Twelve Months

West Marine Inc (WMAR)   MyRollingStocks.com Charts

West Marine, Inc. is a waterlife outfitter for cruisers, sailors, anglers and paddlesports enthusiasts. The company offers a selection of core boating and water recreation products, primarily serving the needs of boat owners and the professionals providing services to them. It services its customers through physical stores and two e-commerce websites. It is a specialty retailer of boating supplies, gear, apparel, footwear and other waterlife-related products. It operates approximately 260 stores located in approximately 40 states, Puerto Rico and Canada. Its products include boating products and merchandise expansion products.

If you have gotten this far in the book, then it must mean that you are both disciplined and patient. A trader who got into WMAR in December would have needed to exercise patience – so this is a fitting place to put WMAR. The stock is trading between a $8 support and a $10 resistance level. As you review the graph, you will note that an investor who got into the stock in December would have to wait until April for the stock to get to the $10 resistance price level. A four month wait is not uncommon with rolling stocks because the rewards are just as satisfying. That four month holding period would have resulted in a $2 gain which is a 25% gain in four months. Not too shabby, eh (as our neighbors up north would say)? WMAR is a great example of a rolling stock. Why? You could have done the same trade again in July and in one month you would have racked up another 25% gain. Oh, and what the heck, just for good measure, you could have done the trade again in October.

WMAR Share Related Items	
Market Cap (Mil) $	234.99
Shares Outstanding (Mil)	24.95
Float (Mil)	16.63
Beta	1.5
Per Share Data	
Earnings TTM	0.2
Sales TTM	28.31
Book Value MRQ	12.73
Cash Flow TTM	1.09

Mil = Million * MRQ = Most Recent Quarter * TTM = Trailing Twelve Months

Those 23 stocks are just a sample of the opportunities that exist with trading rolling stocks. There is more – but of course, it would be voluminous to put it all in one book. So just like the Harry Potter series, watch out for more magic in another book – soon to be published.

"Try a thing you haven't done three times. Once, to get over the fear of doing it. Twice, to learn how to do it. And a third time to figure out whether you like it or not." – *Virgil Thomson*

GLOSSARY

8-K: SEC report required by the Securities Exchange Act of 1934 from public companies announcing unusual material events.

10-K: The SEC annual report required from public companies by the Securities Exchange Act of 1934

10-Q: The SEC quarterly report required of public companies by the Securities Exchange Act of 1934

200 day moving average: Average closing price over the previous 200 days for a stock or an index

401K plan: A qualified defined contribution plan offering of employer-matched contributions.

403B: A qualified plan for tax-exempt non-profit organizations.

404C ERISA: Safe harbor provisions allowing employers to pass off risk to participants of defined contribution plans.

529 saving plans: An education savings plans offering tax deferred growth and tax redistribution at Federal level for qualified education expenses.

ADR: Abbreviation for an American depository receipt, which is a foreign stock on a domestic market.

Advance/decline ratio: The number of stocks whose market prices increased versus the number of stocks whose market prices decreased during a trading session.

Age based portfolio: A mutual fund or other portfolio adjusting asset allocation to match the time horizon needs of the beneficiary

Aggressive growth: Equity investments that face a higher risk of loss but also a higher potential return.

Aggressive investor: An investor willing to risk the large loss of principal in order to earn potentially large returns.

American style option: An option that can be exercised at any time after expiration as opposed to European style.

Annualized return: The rate of return adjusted for increments of one year.

Appreciation: The increase in an asset's value that is not subject to tax until realized.

Arbitrage: A trading tactic that involves taking advantage of the disparity of two assets. For example, if you think MSFT will buy a small company, you can make a bet that MSFT will temporarily drop while the small company's stock will skyrocket.

Ask/Asks: The higher price in a court representing what the customer would have to pay/what the dealer is asking the customer to pay.

Asset allocation: Maintaining a percentage mix of equity, debt, and money market investments based either on the investor's age or market expectations.

Asset: Something that a corporation or an individual owns. Example, cash investments, accounts receivable, inventory, etc.

At the money: An option whose strike price is equal to the market price of the underlying instrument.

Automatic reinvestment: feature offered by mutual funds allowing investors to automatically reinvest dividend and capital gains distribution into more shares of the fund without paying a sales charge.

Bear/Bearish: Investor who takes a position based on the belief of the market or a particular security will fall. Short sellers and buyers of puts are bearish. They profit when stocks go down.

Bear market: A trading market for stocks or bonds in which prices are falling and/or are expected to fall, characterized by a series of low highs and lower lows.

Benchmark: The index to which an investor's manager's results are compared.

Beta: Risk measurement that compares the volatility of a security or portfolio to the volatility of the overall market.

Bid: The amount that a dealer is willing to pay to a customer who wants to sell. Customers sell at the bid, buyers at the ask.

Black-Scholes Equation: The Black-Scholes model is used to calculate the theoretical price of European put and call options, ignoring any dividends paid during the option's lifetime.

Book value or book value per share: the hard-tangible asset value associated with each share of common stock calculated by taking shareholder's equity minus preferred shares divided by the number of shares outstanding.

Bottom up analysis: A type of fundamental analysis involving a look at particular companies rather than the overall economy.

Breakeven: The price at which the underlying security is above or below the strike price of the option by the amount of a premium paid or received. For example, an ABC August 5th call at $2 has a breakeven of $52 for both the buyer and the seller.

Broker: An individual or firm that charges a commission to executive securities' buy and sell orders submitted by another individual or firm.

Bull/Bullish: An investor who takes a position based on the belief that the market or a particular security will rise.

Bull market: A trading environment for stocks and bonds in which prices are rising and/or are expected to rise.

Business cycle: A progression of expansions, peaks, and fractions, troughs and recoveries of the overall micro economy.

Buy and hold: Investment approach that involves holding securities long-term in order to reduce transaction costs and based on a belief that good companies, in general, rise in value over time.

Buy limit: An order to buy a security at a price below the current market price, executable at a specific price of lower or better.

Buy stock: An order to buy a security at a price above the current market price triggered only if the market price hits or passes through the stock price.

Call: Similar to call option, a contract that gives the holder the right to buy something at a stated exercise price.

Call premium: The price paid and received on a call option or the amount above the par value paid by the issuer to call/retire a bond.

Call risk: The risk that a call of a bond or a preferred stock will be forcibly called when interest rates fall.

Call spread: Buying and selling a call on the same underlying instrument where the strike price, the expiration, or both, are different.

Capital appreciation: The rise in an asset's market price, the objective of a growth investor.

Capital gain: The amount by which the proceeds on the sale of a stock or bond exceeds your cost basis. If you sell a stock for $22 and have a cost basis of $10, the capital gain, or profit, is $12.

Capital loss: Loss incurred when selling an asset for less than the purchase price.

Capital risk: The risk that an investor could lose some or all of the investment principal. For securities, investors avoided this only by purchasing US Treasury securities and holding prematurely.

Cash account: An investment account in which the investor must pay for all purchases no later than two business days following a regular way settlement. This is not a margin account.

Cash dividend: A payout to shareholders from an issuer's current earnings or accumulated profits.

Cash flow: Cash flow is the total amount of money being transferred into and out of a business, especially as affecting liquidity

Chart: This is a graphic or representation of a stock's price and value information over time.

Charges: A technical analysis making trading decisions based on stock charge and patterns.

Commodity: A basic raw material used to produce value added products. For example, wheat, corn, oil, sugar, and salt are commodities used to make value added products.

Common stock: An equity or ownership position that allows the owner to quote on major corporate issues such as stock splits, mergers, acquisitions, and authorization of more shares, etc.

Compound interest: An interest rate applied to an ever-increasing principal to which interest is continuously added. Two examples are the rate offered in a bank CD as opposed to simple interest, which is applied to a flat principal, and a long-term bond.

Compound returns: All investors hope to achieve this by reinvesting interest on dividends.

Trade confirmation: Documents stating the trade dates, settling date, and money due/ owed for a securities purchase or sale delivered on or before the settlement date.

Consumer price index: A measure of inflation/deflation for basic consumer goods and services. A rising CPR represents the greatest risk to the most fixed income investors.

Contraction: Phase of the business cycle associated with general economic decline, recession, or depression.

Cost basis: The amount that has gone into an investment that has been taxed already. For stock, this includes the price paid plus commissions. For a variable annuity, this equals the contributions into the account. Investors pay tax only on amounts above their cost basis and only when they sell or take constructive receipt.

Covered call: If an investor already owns the stock, the investor can generate premium income by selling the right to buy stock at a set price.

Day order: A limit or stock order that will be cancelled if not executed on the day it is placed as opposed to a GTC.

Day trading: Purchasing and selling or selling and purchasing the same security on the same day in a margin account.

Debt-to-equity ratio: Measure of long-term solvency found by dividing a company's total liabilities by shareholder equity. The higher the ratio, the more leverage the company has.

Decision Point Price Momentum Oscillator (PMO): is an oscillator based on a Rate of Change (ROC) calculation that is smoothed twice with exponential moving averages that use a custom smoothing process. It can also be used as a relative strength tool.

Derivative: An investment that derives its value from some other instrument.

Dividend: Money paid from profits to holders of common and preferred stock if and when the board of directors declares a dividend.

Dividend Reinvestment Plan, or DRIP: A program allowing investors to automatically reinvest cash dividends into more shares or fractional shares.

Dividend yield: Annual dividends divided by the market price of the stock equivalent to current yield for a debt security.

Dollar cost averaging: Investing fixed dollar amounts regularly regardless of the share price. This usually results in a lower average cost compared to the average of share prices of investors' dollars by a majority of the shares at lower prices. Also, a way of figuring cost basis for income tax purposes, usually called average cost basis.

Dollar weighted return: The rate of return weighted by the dollars invested rather than taking a cent average of all annual returns. It is time weighted return.

Earned income: Income derived from active participation in a business, including wages, salary, tips, commissions, and bonuses. Alimony received is also considered earned income. Earned income can be used toward an IRA contribution.

Earnings per share: The amount of earnings or net income available for each share of common stock.

Ease of Movement (EMV) is a volume-based oscillator that fluctuates above and below the zero line. As its name implies, it is designed to measure the "ease" of price movement.

EBIT: Earnings before interest and taxes. This is the profit that would be shown before interest and taxes are subtracted from revenue on the income statement.

EBITDA: Earnings before interest, taxes, depreciation, and amortization. The profit before interest, taxes, depreciation, and amortization are subtracted from revenue on the income statement.

Efficient market hypothesis: This is an investment approach that assumes markets are efficient with information immediately priced in through the securities.

Emerging market: The financial markets of a developing country, generally a small market with a short operating history not as efficient or stable as developed markets. Brazil, China, India, Russia are considered emerging markets.

Enterprise Value (EV): Enterprise value is equal to the total value of the company, as it is trading on the stock market. To compute it, add the market capitalization and the total net debt of the company.

EV to EBITDA: This is perhaps one of the best measurements of whether or not a company is cheap or expensive. To compute, divide the EV by EBITDA. A higher number signifies a more expensive company.

EV to Sales: This ratio measures the total company value as compared to its annual sales. A high ratio means that the company's value is much more than its sales. To compute it, divide the EV by the net sales for the last four quarters.

Equity ownership: Ownership of common and preferred stock in a public company.

Equity funds: Mutual funds that primarily invest in equity securities.

Equity options: Standardized derivatives giving the holder the right to buy or sell the underlying stock at a set price.

European style option: An option that may be exercised at expiration only.

Ex-date or ex-dividend date: The date upon which the buyer is not entitled to the upcoming dividend.

Exercise: The act of using an option to buy or sell the underlying instrument.

Exercise price: The price at which the underlying security can be bought, in the case of a call, or sold in an options contract. This is also known as the strike price.

Expiration date: The date after which an options contract ceases to exist.

Exponential Moving Average: An exponential moving average (EMA) is a type of moving average that is similar to a simple moving average, except that more weight is given to the latest data.

Fed funds rate: The interest rate charge on bank-to-bank loans subject to daily fluctuation.

Fiduciary: Someone responsible for the financial affairs of someone else.

Financial statement: A balance sheet income statement, statement of cash flows, or other documents showing various aspects of businesses, financial conditions, or results. This is also found in the 10-K or other required reports of public companies.

Footnotes: These are explanatory notes provided to explain financial statements more clearly. For example, accounting methods for inventory or one-time expenses might require further explanation after the numbers are represented in the company's 10-K.

Free cash flow: This tells an investor how much actual cash a company is left with after any capital investments. Positive free cash flow is attractive to investors.

Fundamental analysis: Studying companies in charge of their competitive position and financial strength to determine the advisability of investing in their securities.

Fundamental analyst: An analyst who makes securities investment decisions based on studying the fundamental of the issuer, including financial statements.

GDP: Total goods and services being produced by the economy; economic output, regardless of the nationality of the workers.

GTC, or good until cancelled: A limit or stock order that is to remain open until executed or cancelled by the investor as opposed to a day order, which will be cancelled that day.

Goodwill: Intangible asset representing the price paid to acquire a company above its hard tangible value.

Gross margin: Gross profit divided into revenue. For example, a company with 100 million dollars in revenue and the cost of goods sold of 70 million dollars has a gross profit margin of 30%.

Growth: An investment objective that seeks capital appreciation achieved through common stock.

Growth stock: A stock in a company expected to outperform a market and trading at a high valuation ratio. Example, higher EP ratio.

Head and shoulders: A track pattern used by technical analysts to determine that a bull or bear trend is about to reverse.

Hedge/hedging: To modify the risk taken on a stock position by buying or selling options; for example, a covered call.

Holding period: Period during which a security was held for purposes of determining whether a capital gain or loss is long- or short-term.

Income: Investment objective that seeks current income. This is found by investing in fixed income securities; for example, bonds and money market funds.

Income statement: A financial statement showing a corporation's results of operations over a quarter or a year. It shows revenue, dollar expenses and costs, and the profit or loss the company showed over the period.

Index: Theoretical grouping of stocks and bonds, etc. The Consumer Price Index is a theoretical grouping or basket of things that consumers buy that is used to track inflation.

Index fund: A mutual fund or ETF designed to track a particular index.

Inflation: A loss of purchasing power as measured by the Consumer Price Index.

Interest rate: The charge for borrowing money in a loan. The borrower pays some rate against the principal amount borrowed until the loan is retired. That rate is the interest rate on the loan.

Internal rate of return: In discounted cash flow analysis, the rate of return that makes the net present value of cash flows expected from a project equal to zero. This is also known as the discount rate.

In the money: A call option allowing an investor to buy the underlying stock for less than it is worth, or a put option allowing an investor to sell the underlying stock for more than its worth. For example, if ABC trades at $50, both the ABC October 45 calls and the ABC October 55 calls are in the money.

Investment objective: Any goal that an investor has, including current income, capital appreciation, capital preservation, or speculation.

Investment risk: Factor that can have a negative effect on the overall value of an investment or the income it produces.

Leaps: Leaps are long-term standardized options.

Leverage: Using borrowed money expecting the profits made to be greater than the interest payable.

Liabilities: This is what an individual or a company owes; for example, credit card debt, mortgage balance, or accounts payable.

Limit orders: Orders to buy or sell a security at a specific price or better.

Limited trading authorization: Authorization for someone other than the account owner to enter purchase and sale orders but make no withdrawals of cash or securities.

Liquid net worth: Net worth figured without including hard to sell assets such as real estate or art work.

Long to buy or own: This means to begin a securities transaction by making a purchase.

Long-term capital gain: Profit realized when selling stock held for at least 12 months plus one day.

Margin: Amount of equity contributed by a customer as a percentage of the current market value of securities held in a margin account.

Margin account: Margin account allows investors to engage in short sales and investing foreign money as opposed to a cash account.

Market Cap: This is short for market capitalization. It is the value of all of the company's stock - multiply the current stock price by the fully diluted shares outstanding.

Market order: An order to buy or sell a security at the best available market price.

Minimum maintenance requirement: The minimum amount of equity that a margin customer must maintain on either a short or a long position.

Money market mutual fund: Highly liquid holding place for cash, sometimes called still value funds or as a short share price is generally maintained at a dollar.

Moving Average Convergence Divergence: Moving average convergence divergence (MACD) is a trend-following momentum indicator that shows the relationship between two moving averages of prices.

MyRollingStocks.com: The premier online source to find rolling stocks and information about rolling stocks.

Naked call: A risky proposal whereby you sell a call against securities not yet owned leading to unlimited risk.

Net profit: Another name for net income after tax.

Net profit margin: A company's net income after tax divided by revenue showing the percentage of each dollar of revenue making its way through the bottom line.

Net worth: The difference between assets and liability.

Open Interest: This is the total number of outstanding contracts that are held by market participants at the end of the day.

Option: A derivative giving the holder the right to buy or sell something for a stated price up to expiration of the contract. For example, puts and calls are derivatives, cut options.

Ordinary dividend: A dividend payment that does not receive qualified dividend tax treatment, but it is rather treated as ordinary income.

Ordinary income: Most income received by a tax payer, including salary, wages, bonuses, bond interest, ordinary dividends, etc.

OTC/Over the counter: This is not traded on NYSE but through NASDAQ and also bulletin board and pink sheet stocks.

Out of the money: An Out-of-the-money option gives the holder no benefit because it has no intrinsic value.

Outstanding shares: Number of shares a corporation has outstanding, is used to calculate EPS.

Overbought: A technical analysis term for stocks that are trading near the resistance price.

Oversold: A technical analysis term for stocks that are trading near their support price.

Parabolic SAR: refers to a price-and-time-based trading system. Wilder called this the "Parabolic Time/Price System." SAR stands for "stop and reverse," which is the actual indicator used in the system.

Penny stock: An OTC equity security trading below $5 per share.

Pivot Points: Pivot Points are significant levels chart readers can use to determine directional movement, support and resistance. Pivot Points use the prior period's high, low and close to formulate future support and resistance. In this regard, Pivot Points are predictive or leading indicators.

Portfolio: The combination of investments that an investor owns.

Portfolio income: Income earning through investing in securities, not to be used towards IRA contribution and not off-settable with passive income.

Preferred stock: A fixed income security whose state of dividends must be paid before common stock can receive any dividend payment. This also gets preference ahead of common stock in a liquidation.

Premium: The amount paid to acquire an options contract.

Present value: The value today of an amount of money in the future discounted at some rate of return.

Price-to-put pressure: The market price of a common stock compared to the book value per share.

Price-to-cash ratio: The market price of a common stock compared to the cash flow per share.

Price-to-earnings ratio: The market price of a common stock compared to the EPS of that stock, also known as the PE ratio.

Price/Earnings to Growth ratio: The price/earnings to growth ratio (or PEG ratio), is a modified version of the P/E ratio that also takes earnings growth into account.

Price-to-sales ratio: The market price of a common stock compared to the revenue per share.

Profit: The bottom line of a company's income statement, revenue minus all expenses; also known as net income.

Put: A contract giving the owner the right to sell something at a stated exercise price.

Qualified dividend: A dividend that qualifies for a lower tax rate versus ordinary income.

Range: In a set of numbers, the difference between the lowest and the highest value.

Realized gain: Amount of profit an investor earns when selling a security.

Recession: A significant decline in economic activities spread across the economy lasting more than a few months, normally visible in real GDP, real income, employment, industry production, and wholesale retail prices.

Relative Strength Index (RSI): This is a momentum oscillator that measures the speed and change of price movements. RSI oscillates between zero and 100.

Retained earnings: This is best explained as all the profits of a business that has not been paid out as dividends but rather reinvested into the business as reflected by other balance sheet accounts.

Return of equity: A measure showing how much in profits each dollar of common stockholders' equity generates for the company. That's net income/shareholder equity.

Return on Assets (ROA): Similar to ROIC, ROA, expressed as a percent, measures the company's ability to make money from its assets. To measure the ROA, take the pro forma net income divided by the total assets.

Revenue: The proceeds a company receives on selling products and services, also known as sales or the top line of the income statement.

Risk: The variability/volatility involving investing, typically measured by standard deviation.

Risk tolerance: The ability to withstand fluctuations in principle value due to the investor's time horizon financial stabilities.

Russell 2000: A small capitalization index.

Sector fund: A stock fund that concentrates heavily on a particular industry, for example, a technology fund.

Sector rotating: This is a portfolio management technique that involves selling or underwriting securities of companies in certain areas of economy and buying or over-weighting securities in other areas.

Security: An investment of money subject to fluctuation in value and negotiable/marketable to other investors. Other than an insurance policy or fixed annuity, a security is any piece of secured paper that can be traded for value.

Sell limit: An order to sell placed above the current market price that may be executed only if the bid price rises to the limit price or higher.

Sell stock: An order to sell placed below the current market price activated only if the market price hits or passes below the stock price.

Semi-strong: This is a strain of the efficient market hypothesis that contends that all published information is already priced into a security. This makes excess returns impossible through fundamental analysis.

Short: To begin a securities transaction by selling.

Short sale: A method of attempting to profit from a security whose price is expected to fall. Traders borrow certificates through a broker/dealer and sell them with the obligation to replace them at a later date, hopefully at a lower price.

S&P 500: A large capitalization index that is comprised of the 500 largest companies in the US.

Speculation: High risk investment objective for investors willing to bet on a large price change in an asset respective of any company might produce. Short-term speculators trade options in futures while long-term speculation is in evidence by holding or raw land.

Stochastic Oscillator: The Stochastic Oscillator is a momentum indicator that shows the location of the close relative to the high-low range over a set number of periods

Stock: Ownership or equity position in a public company whose value is tied to the company's profits and dividend pay outs.

Stock dividend: Pay out of a dividend in a form of more shares of stock, not a taxable event.

Shareholders' equity: The difference between a company's assets and liabilities.

Stock split: A change in the number of outstanding shares designed to change the price per share, not a taxable event.

Stock loss: This is another name for a sell stock order, so named because an investor's losses are stopped once the stock trades at a certain price or lower.

Stock order: A securities buy or sell order that is activated only if the market price hits or passes through the stock price, does not name the price for execution.

Stop limit order: A stop order that, once triggered, must be filled at an exact price or better.

Straddle: Buying a call and a put on the same underlying instrument with the same strike price and expiration, or selling a call and a put on the same underlying instrument with the same strike price and expiration.

Strong form: A strain of the efficient market hypothesis that assumes all information, public and private, is already priced into a security.

Technical analyst: Stock traders who rely on market data to support buying and selling opportunities rather than information on companies who issue stock.

Time value: The value of an option above its intrinsic value. For example, if XYZ trades at $50 and XYZ October 5th call at $1 has no intrinsic value but has a $1 of time value.

Time value of money: The fact that a sum of money is worth more now than at some point in the future due to its earning potential.

Time-weighted return: The average of returns over a time period.

Top down analysis: A type of fundamental analysis starting with overall economic trends and then moving down to an industry sector and particular companies.

Total assets: Current assets plus fixed assets plus intangible assets.

Total liabilities: Current liabilities plus long-term liabilities.

Total return: A measure in growth and share price plus dividend and capital gains distribution.

Trade confirmation: This is a document containing details of a securities transaction. For example, price of the security, commissions, stock involved, number of shares, representative code, trade date, and settlement date.

Trade date: The date that a trade is executed.

Trading authorization: This is a form granting another individual the authority to trade on behalf of the account owner.

Trend line: The overall upwards or downwards or sideways price and trade of a stock or index as revealed by a chart.

Unrealized capital gain: The increase in the value of a security that has not been sold. Unrealized gains are not taxable.

Valuation ratio: A comparison of a stock's market price to the EPS, book value, cash flow, or revenue associated with one share of that stock.

Value stock: As opposed to a group stock, a value stock trades at a low PE ratio.

VIX: A key measure of market expectations or near-term volatility conveyed by the S&P 500 stock index option prices. They are both options and futures contracts based on the VIX or [fear 01:00:23] index. The full name is the Chicago Board Options Exchange Market Volatility Index.

Volatility: Up and down movements of an investment that make investors dizzy and occasionally nauseated.

Volume: Total number of shares traded over a given time period.

Wash sale: Selling a security at a loss but then messing up and repurchasing it within 30 days and, therefore, not being able to use it to offset capital gains for that year.

Yield: The income a security produces.

NOTES

1. Justin Fox, *The Myth of the Rational Market,* (Harper Collins Publishers 2009), 231

2. Roger Lowenstein, *When Genius Failed, The Rise and Fall of Long term Capital Management*, (Random House 2000), 188

3. Gregory Witt, *Rolling Stocks Making Money on the Ups and Downs*, (Lighthouse Publishing Group Inc. 1998), 39

www.ingramcontent.com/pod-product-compliance
Lightning Source LLC
Chambersburg PA
CBHW062042200326
41519CB00017B/5106